ILLUSION
AND
DISILLUSION:

THE SELF IN LOVE AND MARRIAGE

John F. Crosby

Indiana University

Wadsworth Publishing Company, Inc.
Belmont, California

Designer: Russ Leong
Editor: Adrienne Harris
Cover: Barbara Ravizza

ISBN-0-534-00225-0
L. C. Cat. Card No. 72-90580
Printed in the United States of America
2 3 4 5 6 7 8 9 10—77 76 75 74 73

ACKNOWLEDGMENTS

American Psychological Association—for excerpts from Harry F. Harlow, "The Nature of Love," *American Psychologist*, Vol. 13, 1958, pp. 673–685. Copyright 1958 by the American Psychological Association; for excerpts from Arthur T. Jersild, "Self-Understanding in Childhood and Adolescence," *American Psychologist*, Vol. 6, 1951, pp. 122–126. Copyright 1951 by the American Psychological Association; and for excerpts from Abraham H. Maslow, "A Theory of Human Motivation," *Psychological Review*, Vol. 50, 1943, pp. 370–396. All these excerpts are reprinted by permission of the American Psychological Association. Appleton-Century-Crofts—for excerpts from *The Family in Search of a Future: Alternate Models for Moderns*, Herbert A. Otto, Editor. Copyright © 1970 by Meredith Corporation. Reprinted by permission of Appleton-Century-Crofts, Educational Division, Meredith Corporation. Columbia University Press—for excerpts from Andreas Capellanus, *The Art of Courtly Love*, abr. and ed., Frederick W. Locke. Copyright 1941 by Columbia University Press. Reprinted by permission of Columbia University Press. W. H. Freeman·and Company—for excerpts from *The Antecedents of Self-Esteem* by Stanley Coopersmith. W. H. Freeman and Company. Copyright © 1967. Reprinted by permission of W. H. Freeman and Company. Harper & Row, Publishers, Inc.—for excerpts from *I'm OK—You're OK* by Thomas A. Harris, pp. 17–18, 19, 20, 25, 26, 29, 32, 46, 48–49, 50 and 52. Copyright © 1967, 1968, 1969 by Thomas A. Harris, M.D. Reprinted by permission of Harper & Row, Publishers, Inc. Holt, Rinehart and Winston, Inc.—for excerpts from *Man for Himself* by Erich Fromm. Copyright 1947 by Erich Fromm. Reprinted by permission of Holt, Rinehart and Winston, Inc. McCall Publishing Co.—for excerpts from Aron Krich and Sam Blum, "Marriage and the Mystique of Romance," *Redbook*, November 1970. Copyright © 1970, McCall Corporation; for excerpts from Margaret Mead, "Marriage in Two Steps," *Redbook*, July 1966. Copyright © 1966, McCall Corporation; and for excerpts from Margaret Mead, "New Designs for Family Living," *Redbook*, October 1970. Copyright © 1970, McCall Corporation. All these excerpts are reprinted by permission of the publisher. William Morrow & Co., Inc.—for excerpts from *The Intimate Enemy* by George Bach and Peter Wyden. Copyright © by George R. Bach and Peter Wyden. Reprinted by permission of William Morrow & Co., Inc. W. W. Norton & Company, Inc.—for excerpts from *The Neurotic Personality of Our Time* by Karen Horney, M.D. Copyright 1937 by W. W. Norton & Company, Inc. Copyright renewed 1964 by Renate Mintz, Brigitte Swarzenski, and Marianne von Eckardt; for excerpts from *Love and Will* by Rollo May. Copyright © 1969 by W. W. Norton & Company, Inc.; for excerpts from *Man's Search for Himself* by Rollo May. Copyright 1953 by W. W. Norton & Company, Inc. All these excerpts are reprinted by permission of W. W. Norton & Company, Inc. Saturday Review, Inc.—for excerpts from Herbert A. Otto, "Has Monogamy Failed," *Saturday Review*, April 25, 1970. Copyright 1970 Saturday Review, Inc. Reprinted by permission of the publisher. Van Nostrand Reinhold Company—for excerpts from *Toward A Psychology of Being* by Abraham Maslow. © 1968 by Litton Educational Publishing, Inc. Reprinted by permission of Van Nostrand Reinhold Company.

Preface

The essays that make up this book are the themes of my lectures in "Marriage and Family Relations" at Indiana University. Existing textbooks and anthologies often attempt to introduce the student to the subject matter in a way that, in the name of academic objectivity, reduces the more subjective aspects of emotionality, meaning, and value to second-rate importance. I have personally grown dissatisfied with such approaches to the subject, for they can reduce the marital relationship to a "something for something" *(quid pro quo)* relationship, a sexual encounter based on method and technique, a utilitarian form of conjugal living that is "best for the kids," or to a residue in the wake of romance.

As Rollo May has pointed out, a writer usually writes because he is struggling with his own thoughts and ideas. Certainly I am! What is said in these pages represents my attempt to weave insights gleaned from the disciplines of psychology, philosophy, sociology, and theology into a cogent whole that can speak to the married and unmarried in more than an academic or intellectual way. I have consciously attempted to avoid bias born of liberal or conservative viewpoints. The one bias that I can do little about stems from my own socialization within the middle-class, white, Anglo-Saxon, Protestant community. It is both easy and fashionable to condemn the "WASP" value system, but it is another thing altogether to try to work through that heritage so that it may become self-corrective and meaningful rather than moralistic and self-imprisoning. Thus, my purpose in this book is to analyze the self in the marital situation and then label as clearly as possible what is myth and nonmyth, self-defeating and self-enhancing, destructive of meaning and productive of meaning. Many may disagree with my analysis and my labeling, but I will gladly take that risk in order to press forward an approach to marriage that centers directly on the human quest for happiness and fulfillment within a framework of value and meaning.

My hope in writing this book is to challenge the reader to think of marriage as a relationship between two people open to change and growth and thus not bound to the imprisoning binds of traditional societal role definition and expectation. If these pages serve to raise one's anxiety level and make one feel uncomfortable, then I am glad, for I fail to see how real change will take place in our societal marital system until people begin to question seriously the premises and assumptions underlying it.

A teacher's manual is available for those who will be working with the ideas and subjects treated in the text. Howard V. Jones of Sacramento City College has done an outstanding job of compiling the resource material. The manual includes my extensive notes on the major ideas in each chapter, as well as further commentary and elaboration of the case study material. In addition, there are suggested projects and exercises for each chapter, a resource section listing slides, films, tapes, and annotated readings, and multiple-choice and essay questions for testing.

I would like to thank

—the students at Syracuse University and Indiana University, who have listened to this material in its lecture format, for their critical comments and suggestions.

—graduate students and associate instructors who have worked with me as discussion leaders in the marriage course. Their insightful questions always served to help me attain a clarity in my own mind, if not always in the text.

—Steve Rutter, Jack Arnold, Harry Campbell, Jan Wosser, and Adrienne Harris of the Wadsworth staff.

—E. H. Brimberry of San Joaquin Delta Community College, Howard V. Jones of Sacramento City College, and Florence Rose of Chaffee College, each of whom contributed immensely to the final manuscript through their written critiques.

—my wife, Marjorie, for the personal gestalt of marriage and shared parenthood.

—the many insightful writers whom I quote and who have influenced my thinking.

Naturally, I take full responsibility for the content of the book and for the interpretations I have placed upon the thought of others.

Contents

FOR:

Rick . . .

Andrew . . .

Scott.

1   Scapegoating Marriage: The Roots of Marital Disillusionment

Does an idealized, romanticized, and sexualized image of marital bliss create a double-bind for married couples? Does the legal-ecclesiastical stance toward the institution of marriage make it into a lifelong contract with no escape clause? To what extent are marriage problems due to the institution and to what extent is the institution used as a scapegoat? To what extent is sex the determiner of the marital relationship? What are the sources of illusion and disillusion in marriage? What alternatives are there to illusion and disillusion?

The Dynamics of Scapegoating

"So what's to get married for?" "Marriage has had it." "The family unit is in a state of breakdown." Such statements are commonplace today. They were also commonplace yesterday—and yesteryear, and at the turn of the century, and before that . . . and . . . and. . . . So what else is new?

Critics of marriage and family life are sometimes prone to blaming certain ideas and practices for all the difficulties associated with marriage and the family. Such doubters offer the following explanations for the breakdown of marriage.

Marriages fail today because of:

Lack of a sense of morality.

Lack of a sense of duty, commitment, and responsibility.

Lack of intestinal fortitude.

The legalization of the marital contract.

The religious belief in indissolubility.

Archaic sexual laws and beliefs.

Archaic definitions of marriage.

Romantic expectations.

Frustration at not finding happiness.

Lack of communication.

The concept of monogamy.

Permissive child rearing.

Sexual repression and inhibition.

Female liberation.

One would question whether these reasons are the real offenders. They may be factors in marriage failures, but it seems that they are being singled out to carry the weight of the whole. In short, these reasons are used as *scapegoats*—they are ascribed blame for the misdeeds or mistakes of others. By definition, a scapegoat is a falsely accused offender. And people seem to make such accusations in order to focus blame or responsibility away from themselves. One need not participate in many bull sessions about marriage and the family before the entire list of scapegoats is brought into the conversation, either directly or by implication.

The scene is a gasoline station. While waiting to have his car greased, Mr. S hears horns honking. Outside he sees a car decorated with tin cans and streamers, followed by three other cars. Mr. T, also waiting for his car, makes the comment, "Some poor guy just made his last will and testament." Mr. S replies, "Yeah, he didn't know when he was well off. If he had stayed single, he could have had everything he wanted, but once you say 'I do'—well, legalizing it kills it." Mr. T counters, "That's because marriage hasn't changed with the times . . . why, my brother-in-law lost his shirt in a divorce case, his wife's attorney really cleaned him. Now, if we weren't hung up on this one-wife business we could come and go in marriage—or have several wives at one time." Mr. S: "Yeah, even the Bible allows for easy divorce and more than one wife. . . ."

In this conversation, which could be overheard at any meeting place, the legal encumbrances have been singled out as scapegoats. Mr. S and Mr. T have convinced themselves that the legal structure is the chief cause of marital misery.

The scene is a luncheon meeting of the mayor's commission for a safer city. Mrs. L is speaking: "The trouble with the world today is that nobody has a sense of responsibility . . . all this talk about sex before marriage, and divorce, why, there's just no morality anymore. It's the parents' fault . . . all this permissive child-rearing nonsense." Mr. M replies: "You're quite right, Mrs. L, we need to return to the good old days when parents knew what it was to struggle and to live only for each other . . . none of that free sex and romantic hanky-panky for them. What kids need today is to learn a little fear, respect, and gratitude, and . . . and . . . and . . ."

And so it goes. Here we see a moralistic type of scapegoating, wherein all the ills of marriage, family, and society are laid at the feet of parents who fail to be strict and authoritarian. If one were to eavesdrop on either of the above conversations for an extended period of time two distinct scapegoating trends would emerge. The first trend would blame the institution of marriage per se, and the second would single out moralistic (not necessarily moral) reasons. The former would more likely be heard among those who are disillusioned, embittered, or feeling somewhat trapped. They would probably consider freedom to be the central issue at stake in marriage. The second trend would be more likely to emerge among those who have emphasized the importance of responsibility rather than freedom in interpersonal relationships. This group can afford to speak with authority, superiority, and smugness because they have made it! Their marriages have

Figure 1–1
Scapegoating: Missing the Mark

endured and, regardless of the quality of their relationships, they feel they have the right to make societal prescriptions and proscriptions.

To reply to these critics, let it be said that while scapegoating is neither honest nor valid, the fact remains that people love to scapegoat! Scapegoating is a game with this prime rule: Always shift the blame away from yourself onto someone or something else. Never accept responsibility for yourself or your own situation. This basic rule is absolutely essential for scapegoaters, simply because the instant they fail to shift responsibility they will be forced to look to themselves.

If one is serious in his attempt to "get at the truth" he will avoid scapegoating. Before making value judgments one must attempt to differentiate among value structures without prejudicing the several positions in either a positive or negative direction. That is, we must first work as scientists—investigating and gathering data—before we arrive at value judgments.

If we are to rid the subject matter of both moralistic and antimoralistic valences, we should consider the following questions:

1. By what criteria is family breakdown determined?
2. By what criteria is marriage failure determined?
3. Is it the institution of marriage that is at fault, or is it the family structure? (Does the coming of children negatively affect the marital relationship?)
4. Is it the differential between expectation and reality which produces disillusionment?
5. Does an idealized, romanticized, and sexualized image of marital bliss create a double bind in which we are entrapped no matter which alternative we choose? Does society create images, standards, and illusions, while the conjugal pairs experience frustration in attempting to live up to these stereotypes?
6. Is it the illusive and ill-defined concept of happiness which leads innocent and naive marriage partners into bitter resentment?
7. Is it the **legal-ecclesiastical*** stance of the American judicial system which makes marriage a lifelong contract with no escape clause? Does this system make it impossible to update or revise the contract without a plaintiff-defendant encounter in court?

---

* Boldface terms are defined in footnotes throughout the text.
Legal-ecclesiastical. Referring to the repository of laws, customs, and traditions which have evolved from the Judeo-Christian tradition and been officially codified in the Anglo-Saxon and American body of law and court system.

8. Is it true that in our education-oriented society we consider education for marriage, family life, and human sexuality to be stupid, silly, and an invasion of domestic privacy? After all, everyone knows that marriage and family living is just "doin' what comes naturally."

9. To what extent are marriage problems due to marriage partners' bringing to the marital union a set of stereotypes, roles, needs, models, idealized images, personality hang-ups, defense and escape mechanisms?

10. Is it possible that the culprit is not marriage at all, but rather the socializing process which we embrace in raising our children?

11. Is it possible that the root cause of our dilemma is an internal emptiness, an existential vacuum within which there is little meaning or purpose to life itself? Does our existential anxiety attach itself to the domestic situation?

12. To what extent is sex the determiner of the marital relationship? Is the area of sexual technology the key to marital happiness? If sensuous woman marries sensuous man will the prospects for marital happiness increase: (a) drastically, (b) somewhat. (c) a little?

13. Is it possible that today's preoccupation with sex belies a fear of emptiness, despair, meaninglessness, and death?

14. To what extent are marriage/family problems related to issues of women's liberation? What implications does **equalitarianism** between the sexes have for the marital and familial relationship? Is it possible for the female to be liberated without the male's also becoming liberated from traditional role expectations and performance?

A study of marriage and family today requires a coming to terms with each of the thoughts implicitly or explicitly stated in the preceding questions. An overall simplistic answer is out of the question. Thus, we should distinguish here between a *moralistic* position and a *moral* position. Moralistic positions are based on traditions and customs which are authoritarian in origin. One does the "true and right" thing because tradition says it is true and right. Conversely, a moral position shuns easy answers and depends on a fact-finding, rational approach to the ethical dynamics of a situation. The two positions are poles apart. By now the reader is aware of my bias toward the latter

---

Equalitarianism. A belief in absolute equality among human beings. Especially referring to equality between the sexes without reservation, condescension, or mental equivocation. (Synonym: Egalitarianism).

approach. Thus, he and the writer are doubly responsible to approach, study, and evaluate the material as critically as humanly possible.

The Institution of Marriage

Marriage is an institution: It has legal definition in the United States, it is protected by the courts, and procurement of a license is a necessary step toward legalization. As an institution, marriage encompasses the full range of ecclesiastical tradition represented in the early colonial days. The roots of this tradition are Judeo-Christian, having been transmitted to us via St. Augustine, the Protestant Reformation, the Council of Trent (the Roman Catholic reply to the Protestant Reformation), and the "Great Awakening" of the American frontier. While many scholars consider Christianity to be antisexual, receiving its major antisexual bias from St. Paul and St. Augustine, it would be more accurate to say that the Christian *tradition* has become rigidly antisexual despite the fact that Jesus gave little indication of being antisexual. St. Paul counseled chastity because of his commitment to the belief that people should be totally freed of earthly ties if they are to give themselves to Jesus (1 Cor. 7:1–9). Marriage, of course, would weaken this commitment. He was also antipermissive about sexual relations outside the marital state; his "sex is OK as long as you are married" position seems to come out most clearly in his advice to his hearers that it was better to marry than to be aflame with passion.

Historically there is little doubt that the Judeo-Christian tradition is essentially antisexual, or at least condescendingly sexual. As will be noted later, Victorianism was the pinnacle of this attitude. It is no small task to determine precisely what effect Victorian thinking had upon marital standards and expectations in the late nineteenth and twentieth centuries in the United States.

The focal point in our analysis of the ecclesiastical tradition, however, is the belief in the indissolubility of the marital union. This belief is not, as in the case of sexuality, a matter of tradition alone. Jesus and Paul were advocates of indissoluble unions except on grounds of adultery. The Old Testament is not so clear about this matter, despite the commandment regarding adultery. Before Moses, there was an acceptance of divorce, and after Moses, **concubinage** and sexual relations with non-Hebrew females were continued. To the ancient Jew, adultery was wrong because it involved taking what right-

---

Concubinage. The practice of keeping a concubine—a woman who shares sexual intimacies with a man or, in some societies, a secondary wife who enjoys protection and support but who lacks primary wife status.

fully belonged to another person (David's encounter with Bathsheba) or what one had no right to take. Thus, the hideousness of the sin of adultery was not the sexual conduct involved but the violation of the property rights of other Hebrews. Also, to the Hebrew the purity of the seed must be protected at all costs; thus, adultery for the Hebrew woman was a more heinous sin than for the man.

Nevertheless, the Judeo-Christian tradition influenced the course of marriage and family relationships as no other single tradition or doctrine did. The legal tradition in both Anglo-Saxon and American expressions has grown up as a stepchild of the Judeo-Christian belief in the indissolubility of marriage.

Sociologists, anthropologists, and historians are fairly well agreed that any society has a vested interest in the mate-selection process and in the establishment of a societal definition of legality in the marital union. The primary reason for this interest is rarely the happiness of the married partners per se but rather a concern that the forthcoming generation be adequately socialized. A legal definition of marriage and a societal dependence upon some form of family structure has proved to be indispensable in all known societies.

Figure 1–2
The Trappings of the Marriage
Institution Tend to Confuse and Separate the Couple

Beyond this practical consideration, all of the states of the United States have traditionally upheld the position regarding the indissolubility of marriage. As has been pointed out, this is not a cross-cultural phenomenon but rather a result of the Judeo-Christian/Augustinian-Western/Puritan-Victorian tradition.

The legal system in the United States has reflected this tradition in its full judicial process for divorce, including a plaintiff, a defendant, a judge, and legal counselors representing the plaintiff and the defendant. Underlying this practice is the assumption that there is a guilty party and an innocent party in the marital dyad; one has been wronged or harmed by the other. Within this system collusion—a couple's agreement to waive the issue of guilt and present the court with a mutual agreement to dissolve their relationship—is illegal.

While other contracts have clauses stating the conditions under which the contract may be dissolved or revised, the marriage contract is indissoluble in most states unless there is a court order following a hearing replete with attorneys, plaintiff, defendant, and judge.

There is much disgust with this system. Nevertheless, the American Bar Association has not been able to arrive at any consensus about how to change it, and until that association changes its position it is unlikely that divorce procedures will change drastically. Meanwhile, issues such as alimony, child support, division of property, and visitation rights for the spouse not retaining custody of the children continue to make the entire system a farce. Lying and perjury are encouraged by the system itself. Legal grounds such as adultery and mental cruelty become catchalls and hence become meaningless. The pre-divorce testimony of many is that they intended to part amicably but that they ended up embittered, vengeful, and hating. Why? Because the two attorneys transformed the proceedings into a contest for money, privilege, and property. Several states have made progress in changing the client-defender nature of the divorce proceedings. Florida's no-fault divorce law is one attempt to remedy this unhappy situation, as illustrated by the following editorial from the *Louisville Courier-Journal.*

To Make Divorce Less Painful

Florida's new "no-fault" divorce law is an intelligent effort to take the conflict and bitterness out of divorce proceedings, and make the painful dissolution of a marriage a little more civilized. In fact, that is how the new law refers to the process—not as divorce but as a dissolution of marriage. And it permits the dissolution without the hurtful and often fraudulent accusations of adultery, cruelty or wrongdoing that most states still demand.

Adultery, cruelty or any of the other legal grounds for a divorce are, after all, merely surface indications of the inability of two people to live together harmoniously. And that is what the law is designed to do—let two people dissolve their marriage when it no longer has any productive meaning. No witnesses will be required to testify to the breakdown, or the evil of either partner. Alimony, available to both man and wife, will be allotted not as a punishment but as a means of allowing the disadvantaged partner to gain a new start. Custody of children will be awarded strictly on the basis of the children's welfare, with both partners regarded as equal claimants.

These provisions make sense. Our divorce laws were intended to protect the sanctity of the home and the welfare of the children by making divorce difficult. As divorce rates show, they have not worked. Instead, they have only made the procedure hurtful and costly, thus impairing the ability of the divorced people to regain a normal life, and taking from them money needed to support the children in a critical period.

There was a time when a woman, in order to protect .herself against the stigma of divorce, needed to prove herself guiltless of wrong, and to show that her husband was at fault. But the stigma is not what it was, and there is no longer any justification for forcing two already anguished people to further embitter, debase or perjure themselves in order to dissolve an already broken and meaningless relationship.[1]

There is little wonder that thousands upon thousands of divorced people attack, criticize, and in other ways try to discredit the institution of marriage. Our feelings are not so much the result of our intellect as of our experiences. When one has gone through the devastation of marital dissolution, is it any wonder that he henceforth places most of the blame for his trouble on "the institution" of marriage? Nevertheless, as pointed out at the beginning of this chapter, we should not be content to single out one major cause and lay all other contributing ills at its clay feet. If we are to conduct a truly critical evaluation of marriage, we can say only that the ecclesiastical-legal definition of marriage and its effect on subsequent enforcement of the martial contract is *one* factor to be examined in our discussion.

Societal Influences

In what ways does society contribute to marital disillusionment? The answer to this question is complex but it is safe to say that society aids and abets marital disillusionment by fostering unrealistic and romantic expectations.

A reading of Andreas Capellanus' *The Art of Courtly Love*, a thirteenth-century statement on the nature of love, should give the reader a historical glimpse of the forerunner of the movement known as romanticism.

> Now let us see in what ways love may be decreased. Too many opportunities for exchanging solaces, too many opportunities of seeing the loved one, too much chance to talk to each other all decrease love, and so does an uncultured appearance or manner of walking on the part of the lover or the sudden loss of his property. Love decreases, too, if the woman finds that her lover is foolish and indiscreet, or if he seems to go beyond reasonable bounds in his demands for love, or if she sees that he has no regard for her modesty and will not forgive her bashfulness. Love decreases, too, if the woman considers that her lover is cowardly in battle, or sees that he is unrestrained in his speech or spoiled by the vice of arrogance.[2]

In the light of such a statement, it is not difficult to understand why Albert Ellis says:

> . . . the general marital philosophy of our society is quite opposed to such acts as lovers limiting the period of their love, becoming varietists, engaging in plural affairs, consciously renouncing their loves, or arranging a suicide pact with their beloveds. Instead we espouse what might be called the most illogical climax to romantic courtship and love: consummation. For sexual and marital consummation indubitably, in the vast majority of instances, maims, bloodies, and finally kills romanticism until it is deader than—well, yesterday's romance.[3]

Our society is the inheritor of the courtly-romantic tradition as well as the Victorian-Puritan tradition—two traditions which appear to be strange bedfellows. Both traditions are essentially antisexual and both emphasize purity of motive and a type of spiritual oneness between lovers. If one looks to the opera, literature, drama, movies, television, magazines, newspapers, and advertising of our past and present, he can see how deeply the concept of romance has influenced our cultural heritage. This heritage is transmitted by our courts, our religious institutions, our educational institutions, and our familial institution.

Societal expectations concerning marriage, especially among the middle classes, include the following: People should marry for love; sex should be an expression of love; lovers should become a fused unity; individual identity should accede to "couple" identity; love will flourish once the right love object comes along; falling in love is the appropriate response to the opposite sex; love conquers all obstacles; love that is genuine need not have any **eros;** love and hate are opposites, and one cannot love if one hates nor hate if one loves; conflict is always destructive and to be avoided; unity implies uniformity; males should be more dominant, females more submissive; "good" women are for marriage—"bad" women are for sex; men enjoy sex—women abide it; men enjoy orgasm—women shouldn't really need it or want it; children strengthen a marriage—marriage without children is abnormal; individual happiness is the supreme goal of marriage; marriage to one person should fulfill all human needs of love, affection, romance, sex, companionship, friendship; marriage should satisfy all domestic, economic, and status needs.

These expectations are not all the result of romanticism nor are they all the result of puritanism. They are, however, the product of a fusing of traditions within American society. When a people embraces a Judeo-Christian cultural heritage, a courtly-romantic view of love, a Puritan-Victorian view of sex, rugged individualism, a belief in laissez-faire self-determinism, a semideistic veneration of the Founding Fathers, and a patriotic idolatry of the flag, God, and motherhood, it is not difficult to understand why or how our societal expectations regarding marriage became so contradictory and naively idealistic.

Eros. Traditionally, the physical love between man and woman. Specifically, an aspect of love characterized by passion, tenderness, communication, commitment, and a desire to give as well as receive, to procreate, to create, and to enhance the partner's humanity.

Socialization

The socialization process cannot and should not be separated from societal expectations inasmuch as the societal expectations effectively determine the customs, mores, beliefs, attitudes, and life style into which the child is indoctrinated. Nevertheless, it is useful to examine the process of socialization as carried out by the institutions of family, education, and religion.

The family is the most powerful socializing agent in society. Each parent brings to a marriage his or her life orientation, life style, value structure, religious-**metaphysical**-existential viewpoints, and personality structure. A marriage is contracted, and children come forth. These children are socialized in the manner in which their parents effectively combine their separate orientations.

The family is the first transmitter of moral values and the various components of the common culture. Thus, children begin to learn sexual and marital roles shortly after birth. This type of learning is not a formal process but rather an internalizing process by which the child copies, imitates, and mimics his parental models. Sex-role typing takes place long before school age. Until the introduction of "GI Joe," it was culturally taboo for boys to play with dolls. Boys don't play with dolls. Dolls are for girls. Brothers don't play with dolls—and fathers don't play with dolls! Boys wear trousers. Girls wear dresses. Boys don't have tops on their bathing suits. Girls (who look just like boys from the waist up until puberty) wear halters or bras! What a mystery. Fathers go away to work; mothers keep house. No wonder advocates of Women's Lib are beginning to recognize that men have to unlearn much of their traditional sex-role typing. New attitudes and feelings about wifing and mothering don't come easily to men who as little boys were exposed to a significant female model who wore dresses, kept house, cooked meals, and waited on everyone.

Early sex attitudes are deeply *internalized;* they are learned on an emotional level so thoroughly that they become a deeply believed and accepted part of the self. If a boy scratches his penis and his mother or father scold him or make remarks about being "dirty," "naughty," "not nice," then an aura of mystery begins to surround this organ of

---

Metaphysical. A philosophical term referring to the study of principles and problems connected with understanding the ultimate source of life and the universe.

his body. Erik Erikson has adequately shown us that shame and doubt develop quite early in a child's life, as do guilt and feelings of inferiority.[4] (Erikson's system is referred to as a **"psychosocial"** system as contrasted with Freud's **"psychosexual"** system. Here again is the stress upon the importance of society and the common cultural tradition. Horney, Fromm, Sullivan, and Adler give ample witness to the influence of societal factors in the socialization process.)

There are several questions we should ask ourselves about the socialization process. Why do many parents resist sharing intimacies with each other when children are present? (What does a child learn when he sees Daddy pat Mommy on the fanny? He might learn that Daddy has fun doing it and that Mommy enjoys it, too.) Why do some parents consider it a virtue not to fight in front of or in the hearing of their children? Could this practice mean that their children will grow up without having any meaningful models to copy? Sometimes in adult life the people who avoid conflict are those who lacked models who faced conflict directly, fairly, and creatively. How many times in the course of a month do marriage counselors and psychotherapists hear their clients say, "My parents never fought and never argued." Such a remark would indicate one of several possible situations: (1) One of the partners usually gave in on all issues; (2) both partners repressed and suppressed their feelings, attitudes, and beliefs; (3) they let it all out when no one was around or behind closed doors. Where did our parents, our grandparents, and our great-grandparents get the idea that conflict was evil and destructive? Where did they learn that honesty is wrong? Yes, wrong! Isn't it one of the greatest acts of hypocrisy to be dishonest by withholding one's thoughts, attitudes, and feelings? Intrapsychic (within one's own psyche) and interpsychic (in a relationship between two people) honesty require—even demand—the facing of conflict.

A society that emphasizes the importance of marriage in socializing its young contradicts its own popular expectations when it makes little provision for formally educating its young in human development, human sexuality, marital preparation, and family development. Thus, the sex-education controversy of recent years may indeed be a good sign. Opponents of functional courses in personality develop-

---

Psychosexual and **Psychosocial.** Abbreviations for the terms "psychological-sexual" and "psychological-social" which are used to refer to a system of thought relating psychological thought to human sexuality and social dynamics respectively.

ment and sex education have considered the teaching of such subjects to be an invasion of domestic privacy. As a society, we have socialized our children into sexual anxiety in the most effective negative way possible: we have taught rigid sex roles and equally ignored sexual dynamics! We educate for the arts, the physical sciences, the social sciences, mathematics, engineering, automobile mechanics, homemaking (cooking, sewing, and nutrition), and physical education: What passes for mental-health education, sex education, and family-life education is a sham in all too many cases. Educational institutions disclaim responsibility in this area, pointing instead to church and family. Increasingly, some religious denominations and persuasions, usually in the more liberal traditions, are seeking to do a viable job. However, conservative and authoritarian traditions continue to contribute to the greater problem by indoctrinating their young in the very tradition (aesthetic and romantic unions, an antisexual stance, and an ethic that places duty—"oughtness" and "shouldness"—above self-fulfillment and **self-actualization**) that places our entire society in its double-bind.

This combined cop-out of educational and ecclesiastical institutions increases the pressure on the family. (The "family" is, of course, a multifaceted term that lumps together the nuclear, the extended, and the one-parent family.) If marriage itself is a dehumanized arrangement, it seems logical to assume that the family also has become dehumanized. What do we mean, "dehumanized"? Dehumanization is the process of depriving us of our essential dignity as individual persons. We become "things"—objects for manipulation and exploitation. In playing roles, we become unreal, false, or inauthentic. The dehumanization of marriage and family is the result of the same double-bind: on the one hand, it is said that marriage is the epitome of human happiness; on the other, marriage is held to be the foundation stone of human misery. There is a conspiracy of dishonesty wherein the brave pretend to be happy and in their pretense disallow the greatest opportunity for human growth. In order for marriage and family life to become humanized, hypocrisy and illusion, pretense and dishonesty must be shed in favor of true relationship that is based on real feelings and conflict resolution rather than on authoritarian traditions.

While parents have effectively ignored education in sexuality, they have socialized (or programmed) their children to adjust, suc-

---

Self-actualization. Similar in meaning to self-fulfillment or self-realization. Refers to the process of bringing out one's human potential.

ceed, produce, and accomplish. (Accomplish what?) Underlying this process is the idea of the "marketing orientation" described by Erich Fromm.[5] Fromm points out that our value and worth as human beings is contingent upon the price our personalities and abilities can command in the marketplace. Since parents often feel guilty about not having "made it" they look to their children to fulfill their own lack of fulfillment. (Be what I never was able to be—make my life worthwhile by making up for my own lack of fulfillment—complete my incompleteness—fill my cup for me because I did not fill it myself.) While in theory no human being should ever or can ever fulfill another's lack of fulfillment, many young people are socialized to make just such an attempt. The parents who socialize and the children who are socialized in this manner are usually unaware of the implications of such programming.

The socialization process undermines one's growth in self-confidence by emphasizing external controls, such as rules, norms, and ethical codes, rather than encouraging the individual's self-discovery. Thus, adult uptightness about drugs, sex, and morals tells us more about the anxiety level of the adult than about the inclinations of the young. Consider the inherent contradictions in the following parent-son interaction:

> The scene is the living room of the Thompson residence. Bill Thompson, age 16, has just asked his father if he can use the car for the evening.
>
> Mr. Thompson responds: "Frankly, I don't see why I should let you take the car. After all, you don't help me keep it clean, wash it, or wax it. When's the last time you even volunteered to put gas in it? Every time you take the car, something goes wrong with it."
>
> "But, Dad, would you please listen to—
>
> "Wait a minute—you listen to me. Your mother and I trust your judgment, you understand, but we just don't think you are ready for the responsibility of taking the car out alone at night."
>
> "In other words, you *don't* trust me."
>
> "Now, Bill, of course we trust you. It's just that you're a little young to handle certain situations."
>
> "Like what?"
>
> "Well, son, if I have to spell it out for you. You're at the age when girls and sex and cars and drugs all seem to go together. It's not that I don't trust *you*—it's the others I'm leery about. You know how disappointed your mother was when she discovered that pornographic

stuff in your dresser drawer. You should be ashamed of yourself, hurting her like that. Seems to me you could show a little gratitude occasionally—we try to give you every advantage . . ."

"I suppose *you* were never curious about what a naked girl looks like . . ."

"That's enough of that kind of talk out of you . . ."

The reader can diagnose the total failure of communication. Why does the father react the way he does? It seems that in a great deal of socializing trust is counseled, yet trust is withheld. Love is extolled, yet love is used as a shaming technique. Honesty is ritualized, yet honesty is replaced with hypocrisy, for people fear what honesty might reveal to the children—namely, that mother and father are two human beings, fallible, weak, strong, dependent, autonomous (self-sufficient), loving, hostile, selfish, selfless, self-loving, and self-devaluating.

The socialization process within the family is cyclical, in that the transmission of myths, folklore, and expectations is self-perpetuating; unless the pattern is broken, it will be imposed upon one's children, and they in turn will transmit it to their children. Talcott Parsons has suggested that the *superego* (sometimes loosely defined as the conscience) is formed not merely from the internalization of parental standards, but also from the various beliefs, norms, tenets, folklore, taboos, and standards of the common culture:

> If the approach taken here is correct, the place of the superego as part of the structure of the personality must be understood in terms of the relation between personality and the total common culture, by virtue of which a stable system of social interaction on the human level becomes possible. Freud's insight was profoundly correct when he focused on the element of moral standards. This is, indeed, central and crucial, but it does seem that Freud's view was too narrow. The inescapable conclusion is that not only moral standards, but *all the components of the common culture* are internalized as part of the personality structure.[6]

From what we have said about the socialization process so far, it should seem apparent that a large part of the process is the teaching and learning of roles. Roles are usually learned in pairs and clusters rather than singly. That is, as a child learns what it means to be a little boy, he also learns what it means to be a little girl. Fathering roles depend on mothering roles and vice versa. Husbanding roles depend on wifing roles and vice versa. The learning of roles and role expectations is stressed, as Parsons points out, by all the components of the common culture. While the primary group (the family) is most instrumental during the very early years, there is danger in not recognizing the powerful influence of these other cultural components—such as educational institutions, organizations like Boy Scouts, Girl Scouts, men's lodges and service clubs, women's auxiliaries, religious institutions, and civic and political institutions.

This discussion of socialization and its effect on marital disillusionment should clarify the kind of hierarchy of expectations we work with: marital disillusionment is partly due to unrealistic expectations; such expectations are due to one's socialization; socialization in turn is the product of the society and its traditions.

Personality and Character Orientation

The fourth source of marital disillusionment is intrapsychic in nature. Not only do we need to look at role analysis and the sex-role typing which is culturally transmitted, but we also need to look at what psychic needs people expect the marital situation and the spouse to meet for them.

Erich Fromm has described four basic character orientations which seem to predominate among people. These character orientations are important in marriage because they determine the nature of the needs a person brings to the marriage and, consequently, one's expectations for the partner. Each orientation has a common payoff—a sense of intrapsychic security—security within oneself. The goal is to allay anxiety and depression, meaninglessness and emptiness, dread and guilt. But at what price? Usually at the price of satisfactory marital relationships.

The primary trait of the individual with a *receptive orientation* is dependence. He looks to others to take care of him and meet his needs. Freud's **oral phase** of development is marked by traits similar to those of the receptive character orientation. The receptive person

---

Oral phase. The first phase of personality development postulated by Freud, during which the mouth is the primary erogenous zone through which the child gratifies himself and experiences pleasure. As personality develops, oral characteristics may manifest themselves in the form of mouth-centered pleasure.

needs to please others, never wants to offend, needs constant reassurance, and represses feelings of anger, resentment, and hostility. He gains security by submission to authority. His feelings of self-worth depend on other people's view of him. Because he does not have much genuine self-esteem, he depends on others to dote on him, give him succor, praise, and accolades. He is afraid of risk because he lacks confidence in himself. Consequently, he is more likely to be a follower than a leader. At heart he does not trust in his own powers nor does he accept himself in a thoroughgoing way.[7] Karen Horney describes the same personality as one who moves "toward" others.[8]

A person with a fairly strong receptive orientation will place many unrealistic demands on the marital partner. Implicit in these demands will be the same request posed many different ways: "Take care of me; I'm so helpless. I need you in order for me to be me. Reassure me. Don't fight with me, I can't stand conflict. I trust you implicitly to be right . . . and (sensed but never spoken) I'm afraid to disagree with you because you won't love me anymore." A receptive person is not at all without power—his is the power of manipulation through helplessness. The predictable result of the normal-receptive marriage is that the normal will tire of his mate's dependency and gradually feel resentment and a falling out of love.

Fromm's second type of character orientation is *exploitative.* The exploitative traits are akin to the characteristics of the **anal phase** described by Freud. The exploitative person gains security by being "one-up" or "over" others. He cannot tolerate equality because he needs to retain the feeling of power and control so that he himself will not be controlled or manipulated. He is manipulative and sometimes ruthless in his attempts to maintain control. Karen Horney describes this type of person as moving "against" others.[9]

People who reveal marked tendencies to dominate threaten the happiness of any relationship, and certainly a marriage relationship. The implicit and explicit message is always a variation of the theme "Be what I want you to be; do what I want you to do. Live, think, act, breathe the way I tell you. I am right. I am leader. You are less—not quite a person. If you forget who you are and what your position is,

---

Anal phase. Freud's second phase of development, which is characterized by the child's concern and attention on the anus and toileting habits. Anal personality traits are considered to be cleanliness, obstinacy, orderliness, and a desire to hold onto and possess.

you will threaten me for I cannot tolerate insubordination. I demand your love." The outcome of the exploitative-normal match is identical to the receptive-normal—chaos, disillusionment, falling out of love, resentment, and dehumanization.

A third type of orientation is characterized by *hoarding.* According to Fromm, "This orientation makes people have little faith in anything new they might get from the outside world; their security is based upon hoarding and saving, while spending is thought to be a threat." [10] Since love is essentially a possession, the hoarding personality is generally incapable of granting freedom and independence to the beloved. The "saving" characteristic also manifests itself in holding onto memories of the past, collecting things, and clinging to orderliness and punctuality. Somewhat paralleling this concept, but not really similar, is Karen Horney's concept of moving "away" from people. [11]

A hoarding-normal match can be destructive because of the hoarder's overpossessiveness, jealousy, and sometimes extremely conservative attitude toward money and other possessions. A hoarder needs to be constantly reassured of love, never feels sated and hence never really learns to trust in himself as lovable, no matter what reassurance he gets from his partner. This type of relationship can also get locked in a financial squeeze play due to the fact that the hoarder simply cannot part with the symbol of his security—his money.

The fourth type of orientation is the "marketing" orientation. Fromm said of this orientation: "In order to understand its nature one must consider the economic function of the market in modern society as being not only analogous to this character orientation but as the basis and the main condition for its development in modern man." [12] Briefly, the individual possessing a marketing orientation allows his value to be determined by his exchange value in the marketplace. Instead of valuing himself as a unique and worthwhile individual, he allows the market to do the "valuating." That is, he is likely to base his identity on his success in the world of business, sales, industry, commerce, and politics. He may depend a great deal on the role he fulfills and the status he commands, thus attempting to create a locus of worth essentially outside of himself. Rollo May has given an example of this process:

> For example, there is the curious remark made regularly nowadays at the end of radio programs, "Thanks for listening." This re-

mark is quite amazing when you come to think of it. Why should a person who is doing the entertaining, who is *giving* something ostensibly of value, thank the receiver for taking it? To acknowledge applause is one thing, but thanking the recipient for deigning to listen and be amused is a quite different thing. It betokens that the action is given its value, or lack of value, by the whim of the consumer, the receiver—in the case of our illustration, the consumers being their majesties, the public.[13]

This loss of a sense of self runs through the marketing orientation. In our society it is little wonder that retirement for men and the "empty nest" for women are such threatening and often disillusioning experiences. Because their identity as persons has been co-opted from their station, role, status, and salary, they are at a loss to create a new center within themselves.

The marketing-normal match is the most difficult to uncover due to its subtlety and its status as a "culturally patterned defect." Nevertheless, the person with this orientation finds his/her value only in the worth the marketplace ascribes to him/her. Thus, he is more likely to seek his identity in the work world than to place importance on achieving a fulfilling marital relationship. Whenever a marriage partner depends on what value others ascribe to him rather than on his own sense of self-valuation, the result is bound to be a weakening and deterioration of the marital relationship whenever the expected valuation from the marketplace is not forthcoming. Because he lacks inner feelings of self-acceptance and self-fulfillment, his marriage will also be unfulfilling for both him and his partner.

Marital disillusionment can rarely be attributed to a simple or singular factor such as the institution, society, socialization, or personal needs, and character orientation. Rather, combinations and interacting effects join forces to create a feeling of disillusionment— sometimes mild, sometimes severe, and often repressed. The roots of marital disillusionment are powerful and sufficient to create inner feelings of guilt, anxiety, disappointment, misery, and depression. A prescription for treatment would require an honest evaluation of oneself and one's implicit and explicit expectations in light of the institutional, societal, and socialization traditions and practices so prevalent today.

As we have seen in examining Fromm's postulated character orientations, and as we shall see in the next chapter, the net effect of expecting a mate to meet one's illegitimate ego needs is to drive the mate into the unfulfilling position of "deficit-filler."

2 The Happiness Thing: Need Fulfillment in Marriage

What is happiness? What is pleasure? Can pain be the result of joy? What kinds of needs can one reasonably expect to be filled by another person? Are illegitimate needs necessarily bad? To what extent does the endurance of a marital relationship reflect marital happiness? Can one distinguish between mature love and immature love? Is there only one kind of "true love"?

Marital Expectations

People generally expect that marriage will satisfy most of their basic needs. They expect their partner to meet their physical needs, their affect needs, their romance needs, their communication needs, their sharing needs, their sexual needs, their economic needs, and their social needs. There are few societies, if any, that expect as much from the marriage relationship as ours does.

Our children are socialized in such a way that the marital expectations are entirely out of proportion to a realistic assessment of the marital situation. The mass media place marriage on a pedestal and bemoan divorce, idolize sex yet refuse to educate for human sexuality, glorify romance yet insist that romance is for the young and immature. We learn roles from the time we are infants. We internalize the teachings and examples of our role models, who during the first years of our lives are almost exclusively our parents. We build up an **ego-ideal** of ourself and at the same time build up an ego-ideal of a future spouse. In the light of role learning, ego-ideals, mate ideals, cultural expectations, and romantic longings, it is little wonder that the divorce rate is high; in fact, perhaps we should be asking why it is not higher.

Ego-ideal. An idealized image of oneself that is indicative of the way a person would like to be. The ideal self. The fantasied self-image as contrasted with the actual self-image.

Happiness and Pleasure

Young people frequently (if not always) maintain that their chief goal or desire in married life is happiness. Happiness is the great "god" of married life. "We want happiness together more than anything else."

Of course, why not? Everybody wants to be happy. Madison Avenue knows this quite well. Happiness is a trip to Hawaii. Happiness is a bottle of this or a taste of that. Happiness may be a new husband, a new wife, a new sex partner, a new car, a new snowmobile, a new garden tractor. Madison Avenue isn't dumb. There is no doubt that the advertising industry is quite aware that most Americans are restless most of the time, that they nurse feelings of disappointment and disillusionment, that they are largely unfulfilled and non-self-actualizing.

Aristotle (the early Greek who liked to think) has identified happiness in somewhat different terms from those of Madison Avenue. Aristotle referred to happiness as a state of self-fulfillment. W. T. Jones, summarizing Aristotle's thoughts about happiness writes:

> Pleasure is the name we give to immediate satisfaction, which is all that is open to the animal. Happiness is the name for that longer range, more complete satisfaction which reason gives us the possibility of achieving . . . the possibility of more ignominious failure than any animal has experienced is the risk the rational soul must run for the possibility of a much greater fulfillment. . . . Happiness, then, is what we experience when we are virtuous, i.e., when we are living at our best and fullest, when we are functioning in accordance with our nature, when our end is realizing itself without impediment, when our form is becoming actual.[1]

Note the phrases "living at our fullest," "functioning according to our nature," "realizing ourself," and "form becoming actual." This same emphasis is being heard today from people in many different disciplines. Abraham Maslow writes: ". . . for writers in these various groups, notably Fromm, Horney, Jung, C. Buhler, Angyal, Rogers, and G. Allport, Schachtel, and Lynd, and recently some Catholic psychologists, *growth, individuation, autonomy, self-actualization, self-development, productiveness, self-realization,* are all crudely synonymous, designating a vaguely perceived area rather than a sharply defined concept."[2]

A line can be drawn from Aristotle to the present concept of self-actualization. People may quarrel about formal definition, but the essentials of the concept seem quite clear. There is more than a theoretical relationship between happiness and self-actualization: It is a *functional* relationship on the level of feelings, attitudes, values, and behavior, and its focal point is the self-concept. That is, self-actualization constitutes the emotional freedom and autonomy so necessary as breathing space for the human psyche. Without space and freedom to evolve, the psyche becomes stymied, constricted, blocked, and shut in on itself, thus depriving the person of the basic ingredients of happiness.

There is, however, a conceptual and theoretical difference between happiness and pleasure. Can a happy person experience tragedy and grief, yet remain an essentially happy person? Can an unhappy person experience pleasure and joy, yet remain basically an unhappy person? Answer: Yes, in both cases. Why? Because we are talking about two different things. Many essentially happy people go through tragedy and sorrow. Experiencing these feelings does not mean that their personality makeup will be significantly altered. Nor is a little pleasure for an unhappy person likely to significantly change his basic personality. Following this line of reasoning, let us ask, "What words may be used to describe the polar opposite of happiness and the polar opposite of pleasure? Figure 2–1 pictures two intersecting continuum —one axis polarizes happiness, the other polarizes pleasure. There is room for a wide range of possibilities on each continuum.

Both continuums are concerned with affect (emotions). Yet there is a difference between the continuums. The "Happiness-Unhappiness" continuum reflects a state of being which is more or less constant—that is, it is an ongoing, continuous inner state subject to mild mood fluctuations yet relatively constant. The "Pleasure-Sorrow" continuum reflects a different quality of feeling based on periodic or fleeting experiences. The very nature of a peak experience or of a joyful feeling is that it waxes and wanes. Sorrow and sadness likewise come and go. They are not normally thought of as permanent, ongoing states of emotion.

In the light of this discussion about happiness we return to the question of marital goals: Is it logical and rational for people to expect happiness in marriage? The answer is, of course, yes and no.

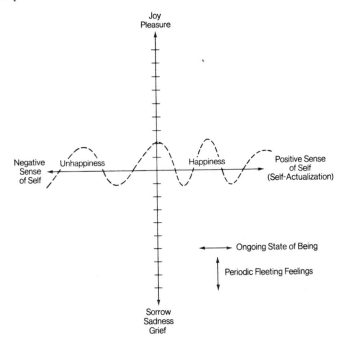

Joy
Pleasure

Negative Sense of Self   Unhappiness   Happiness   Positive Sense of Self (Self-Actualization)

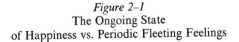

Ongoing State of Being

Periodic Fleeting Feelings

Sorrow
Sadness
Grief

Figure 2–1
The Ongoing State
of Happiness vs. Periodic Fleeting Feelings

Legitimate and Illegitimate Needs

Aron Krich has said, "For marriage will not make an unhappy person happy. Marriage is the relationship that most adults find conducive to attaining satisfaction from life, but marriage in itself does not create happiness. . . . Marriage can add to one's feeling of self-worth if one enters it feeling worth loving in the first place. But the love of a husband or wife cannot make up for the love one failed to get as a child. Countless people approach marriage counseling complaining of the inadequacy of their spouse's love, when actually no amount of love would be enough to make them feel good about themselves." [3]

If a person is essentially a happy person, he or she will not seek a marital partner to make up for a love deficit. The needs that one partner expects the other partner to fulfill will be reasonable—that is, they will be needs that have a rational basis. Among these needs one could list sharing, communication, friendship, erotic love, and nonerotic love. These needs are legitimate in that they are ongoing "being" needs—that is, they are needs that must be filled in present situations in order to sustain an ongoing state of happiness. If, however, a person is a bottomless well of these needs owing to previous deficiencies in his development, one can consider his needs illegitimate. Thus, an illegitimate need is one which is out of balance with reason in that it arises due to deficits in one's prior years rather than from a present realistic situation. If a person has never had the security of perceiving that he was loved and thus has an insatiable desire for reassurance, he may, in effect, be saying to his spouse, "Please love me and make me feel loved (even though I don't really feel lovable)."

Erich Fromm has described the difference between love based on legitimate needs and that based on illegitimate needs. For the person who is mature in his love:

> To give has become more satisfactory, more joyous, than to receive; to love, more important even than being loved. By loving, he has left the prison cell of aloneness and isolation which was constituted by the state of **narcissism** and self-centeredness. He feels a sense of new union, of sharing, of oneness. More than that, he feels the potency of producing love by loving—rather than the dependence of receiving by being loved—and for that reason having to be small, helpless, sick—or "good." Infantile love follows the principle: *"I love because I am loved."* Mature love follows the principle: *"I am loved because I love."* Immature love says: *"I love you because I need you."* Mature love says: *"I need you because I love you."* [4]

Illegitimate ego needs may be described as arising primarily from the insecurity of not "feeling loved" in early childhood, late childhood, and adolescence. The experience of "being in love" is often an emotional response to someone who is perceived as capable of meeting any unmet or partially met needs that we have brought with us from our earlier development. When this is the case, "I love you because I need you" accurately describes the condition of illegitimate need fulfillment. Let us ask what happens when a person loves because he needs. For a while things may go well, but if the spouse is relatively stable and secure he or she will eventually tire of being leaned upon. One day our friend who "loves because he needs" will perceive that he no longer loves his spouse. He will wonder why. "I am falling

---

Narcissism. An exaggerated concern with the self implying a "being in love with" oneself. Not to be confused with self-love or self-esteem.

out of love." "My love has died." In reality the stable, secure spouse has slowly tired of treating the dependent one as a child, of being leaned upon, and of assuming the position of a mother or father substitute. When the dependent subject begins to feel that love is dying, he is actually experiencing his spouse's inability to meet his illegitimate need demands.

If both partners enter a relationship with an "I love you because I need you" orientation, then there is a symbiosis. That is, they share a mutual dependency which makes it impossible for either to function alone in a truly self-fulfilling, mature manner. Thus, a symbiotic relationship is to be distinguished from a genuinely healthy *interdependent* relationship. A symbiotic relationship is built around a mutual meeting of *illegitimate* needs, whereas genuine interdependency is based on a mutual meeting of *legitimate* needs. Paradoxically, symbiotic marriage relationships quite frequently endure. Because both partners experience satisfaction in meeting the illegitimate needs of the other and in turn receive gratification of their own illegitimate needs, they have a basis for an enduring relationship, however immature and neurotic it may be.[5] There is, however, no such thing as a *half-symbiosis!* If only one partner leans toward or upon the other, it is not a symbiosis. A symbiosis, by definition, means that both partners are illegitimately dependent on each other. If only one partner displays these characteristics chances for the marriage's survival are slim, unless the dependent partner can "work through" his dependency in counseling or psychotherapy.

Case Study 1

Ron and Judy have been married for seven years. Judy has had an increasing awareness that she is not happy, and she and Ron have separate appointments with the same counselor.

Judy: "I feel sort of—well, sort of blah most of the time: It's to the point where I only feel happy when we go somewhere special, like to a party. Sometimes I go shopping, just because it makes me feel better. Ron used to make me happy but he seems to be a drag. I love him; but we just don't seem to have any spark left in our marriage. He keeps telling me that I need to get out of myself more—and I'd like to but I don't know how. If only we had more money, then we could do more things together and enjoy life a little. I've thought of getting a job—and I might just as soon as Suzie reaches first grade. Then both children will be in school and I'll have more freedom. Maybe then I'll be happy. Ha! (long pause) I really feel it's Ron's fault. We both agreed when we got married that the most important thing we wanted was happiness. That's a laugh!

Ron: "I don't know what it is with her, but lately I feel totally frustrated. She seems depressed, low—and always expecting me to pull her up. We've spent money like crazy—buy this, buy that, go here, go there: Yet—nothing seems to make her happy. We have sex about twice a week and I enjoy it—and she seems to—but then, she's still miserable. I suppose I should have been more encouraging when she mentioned she would like to get a job. I'm not against it— although I admit I'm not crazy about the idea. It's starting to get me down. I've thought of divorce and of having relationships with other women. But . . . I guess I'm worn down too—I keep feeling guilty because I can't make her happy. There are times I just have to push all my feelings into the back of my mind. I wonder if I even love her anymore."

Ron and Judy cannot be analyzed on the basis of such short statements, but for our purposes it is sufficient to point out the probability that Judy's unhappiness (restlessness, depression) is not the result of Ron's attitude and behavior. Judy's problem lies within Judy. She would feel so much better if Ron would make her happy, but it is not within Ron's power as a human being to fill the unfulfillment of Judy. Judy appears to be an emotionally dependent person who expects her husband to make her happy. This expectation is illegitimate; it can be safely assumed that her present unhappiness stems from emotional deficits she experienced as a child.

The Neurotic Need for Affection

Karen Horney has contributed to our understanding of legitimate and illegitimate ego needs by reviewing the characteristics and attributes of the neurotic need for affection.

Although it is very difficult to say what is love, we can say definitely what is not love, or what elements are alien to it. One may be thoroughly fond of a person, and yet at times be angry with him, deny him certain wishes or want to be left alone. But there is a difference between such circumscribed reactions of wrath or withdrawal and the attitude of a neurotic, who is constantly on guard against others, feels that any interest they take in third persons is a neglect of himself, and interprets any demand as an imposition or any criticism as a humiliation. This is not love. . . . Of course we want something from the person we are fond of—we want gratification, loyalty, help; we may even want a sacrifice, if necessary. And it is in general an indication of mental health to be able to express such wishes or even fight for them. The difference between love and the neurotic need for affection lies in the fact that in love the feeling of affection is primary, whereas in the case of the neurotic the primary feeling is the need for reassurance, and the illusion of loving is only secondary. Of course there are all sorts of intermediate conditions.

If a person needs another's affection for the sake of reassurance against anxiety, the issue will usually be completely blurred in his conscious mind . . . all that he feels is that here is a person whom he likes or trusts, or with whom he feels infatuated. But what he feels as spontaneous love may be nothing but a response of gratitude for some kindness shown him or a response of hope or affection aroused by some person or situation. The person who explicitly or implicitly arouses in him expectations of this kind will automatically be invested with importance, and his feeling will manifest itself in the illusion of love. . . . Such expectations . . . may be aroused by erotic or sexual advances, although these may have nothing to do with love.[6]

It is imperative to underline Horney's remark that there are "all sorts of intermediate conditions." [7] The question of legitimate and illegitimate ego needs is not a question of "either-or" but rather a question of degree.

The extremes are relatively uncommon. The situation is not one of black or white, but intermediate shades of gray. That is, most of us have mixtures of both legitimate and illegitimate ego needs and the point to be emphasized is the degree of the mixture (see Figure 2–2 for representation of various mixtures). There is a point at which, even though the illegitimate needs are present and operating, they may be handled without too much stress being placed on the marital relationship. Beyond this point everything is to the good, with increasing degrees of legitimate ego needs prevailing (see Figure 2–2).

Deficiency Needs and Being Needs

Abraham Maslow offers us a third way of looking at legitimate and illegitimate needs. His concept of "deficiency" needs (D-needs) and "being" needs (B-needs) comes very close to our distinction be-

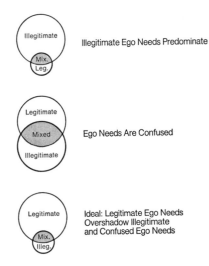

Figure 2–2
The Degree of Mixture
of Legitimate and Illegitimate Ego Needs

tween legitimate and illegitimate ego needs. Maslow outlines four deficiency or "D-needs" which are *prepotent* in nature—that is, they are basic needs which must be met before a person seeks fulfillment of less basic needs.[8] The higher or more elementary the need, the stronger its power, force, or influence. According to Maslow, the following make up the hierarchy of D-needs: (1) physical needs, such as food, drink, sleep, warmth; (2) needs for psychological and physical safety from harm; (3) the need to be loved; and (4) the need for esteem, both self-esteem and that bestowed by others. A person may be operating fairly effectively in meeting his esteem needs, but if he were suddenly cast adrift in a lifeboat in the Pacific Ocean his esteem needs would be of no importance because he would revert to his prepotent physical needs and safety needs. Many times we appear to function at a given level when we are actually trying to make up for a deficiency on the prior level. A person may work diligently for esteem satisfaction, when, in fact, he suffers from a deficiency in being loved, the preceding level. Another may appear to seek satisfaction of love needs when in reality he has never had the prior need of psychological safety fulfilled.

Each D-need must receive *some degree of satisfaction* before a person can move up the ladder to the next need. Any level may collapse at any time due to specific circumstances and crises. When the four levels of the D-needs have been reasonably well satisfied, the individual is able to proceed to the being needs, or the "B-needs." The B-needs constitute what Maslow calls self-actualization:

> . . . the desire for self-fulfillment, namely, . . . the tendency for one to become actualized in what he is potentially. This tendency might be phrased as the desire to become more and more what one is, to become everything that one is capable of becoming. . . . The clear emergence of these needs rests upon prior satisfaction of the physiological, safety, love, and esteem needs. We shall call people who are satisfied in these needs basically satisfied people, and it is from these that we may expect the fullest (and healthiest) creativeness. . . . In actual fact, most members of our society who are normal are partially satisfied in all their basic needs and partially unsatisfied in all their basic needs at the same time. A more realistic description of the hierarchy would be in terms of decreasing percentages of satisfaction as we go up the hierarchy of prepotency. For instance, if I may assign arbitrary figures for the sake of illustration, it is as if the average citizen is satisfied perhaps 85 per cent in his physiological needs, 70 per cent in his safety needs, 50 per cent in his love needs, 40 per cent in his self-esteem needs, and 10 per cent in his self-actualization needs.[9]

Maslow's D-needs are needs which have to be satisfied in some manner, regardless of why they are still unsatisfied. These D-needs are illegitimate because they arise from a developmental deficit, and the responsibility for their fulfillment is thrust upon another person. Unfortunately, the person who most often inherits this cast-off responsibility is the spouse.

William Glasser has pointed out that whenever we look to others to do what we ought to be doing for ourselves we are, in effect, shifting responsibility for ourselves onto the other person.[10] The individual who accepts his own deficiency needs and becomes aware of his own ploys, methods, and strategies to get others to fulfill his own lack of fulfillment is in a position to begin to deal with his own deficiency needs. Then he need no longer play the game of shifting responsibility upon others, which Eric Berne and Thomas Harris have described as

"Look what you made me do," or "Look what you did to me." [11] It could also be described as "Be what I need you to be."

Conjugal Interdependency

The reader is asking, "Isn't it right to expect the mate to meet the needs of the spouse?" Of course! Rational needs that result from mutual interdependency should claim the conjugal help of the mate. If love is the kind of love which says, "I need you because I love you," then for a certainty we may expect mutual need satisfaction. Legitimate ego needs arise from a commitment born of trust, honesty, freedom, and caring. Illegitimate ego needs are born of dependency and an unconscious desire to make another person responsible for "Who I am."

Love based on legitimate needs implies an "active concern for the life and the growth of that which we love." [12] Love based on illegitimate needs does not encourage the growth, freedom, fulfillment, and actualization of the spouse. Legitimate love implies responsibility for the beloved; illegitimate love implies a deterioration of responsibility into manipulative domination and possessiveness. Legitimate love implies respect for the beloved as he or she is; illegitimate love implies "oneness" with the other in the exploitative sense of needing "him to be as an object for my use." [13] Legitimate love implies a knowledge of the other which transcends the concern for oneself; illegitimate love implies a knowledge of the other gained by self-preoccupation—that is, knowledge of the other as a means of having power over him.

Case Study 2

Phil and Sandy have been married two years and they have a one-year-old daughter. Phil sought out a psychotherapist, and explained his situation.

"I came here because I'm afraid I am doing some things that are hurting my relationship with my wife. I might be mistaken . . . (pause) . . . but—I mean to say, it might be a mutual marital problem—but I really don't think so. I keep on finding fault with Sandy —over little things. At times I am beastly to her . . . almost like it's her fault I am me. I get angry and I feel resentment. Its always over little things. She doesn't do the things I think she ought to do. She irritates the hell out of me sometimes. Like the other day—I really wanted her to make over me a little and when she didn't I felt hurt— then I got angry. Later I felt depressed and I kept thinking it was all her fault. It's often that way. I seem to be picking at her about little things and afterwards I resent her all the more . . . (long pause) . . .

and yet deep down I feel that I'm being unfair because she can never win! It's like something inside of me keeps coming out on her. . . . Do you follow what I'm saying? It's almost like she's responsible for the way I feel . . . it's her fault and I take it out on her."

This case study has many possible dynamics, including role definition, role expectation, displacement of anger, internal conflict, and anxiety-hostility. Basically, Phil has correctly sensed a contradiction in himself, and he is correct (on the basis of the evidence presented here) in concluding that this is more *his* problem than his *and* Sandy's problem. Phil resembles the passive-aggressive personality that characteristically expresses aggression in mildly safe, passive ways. The real target of Phil's anger may or may not be Sandy, but he behaves in such a way as to hold her responsible for whatever it is that bugs him. In essence, Phil is shifting responsibility for himself to Sandy, making her the target of his inner hostility-anxiety. In the passive-aggressive framework there is no way for Sandy to win. The problem is Phil's and he would probably benefit himself and the marriage if he could discover the true source of his inner anxiety-hostility. Discovery alone is usually not sufficient to change behavior, but *until* a person gains some insight into his maladaptive behavior patterns he or she is usually unable to identify the concrete changes that need to be made.

In Phil's case, his illegitimate demands on Sandy result from internal anxiety-hostility. When he feels and expresses anger and resentment toward Sandy, it is as though he is condemning her for not being what he wants her to be and for not doing what he wants her to do. Thus, Phil dehumanizes Sandy by focusing on feelings based only on his illegitimate ego needs and bypassing feelings based on an understanding and acceptance of her as she really is. Phil's reaction is bound to be increasingly resentful and, if he had not sensed it in himself, would likely have led to three things: (1) Sandy would eventually tire of Phil's unreasonable and illegitimate demands because she would come to realize that no human being can supply the insatiable quality of Phil's developmental deficits; (2) Sandy would "fall out of love" with Phil simply because his behavior would eventually destroy her positive regard for him; (3) Phil would be likely to conclude that he no longer loved Sandy because she was unable or unwilling to meet his (illegitimate) needs. To the extent that Phil loved Sandy because he needed her he would experience love turned to resentment.

The Origin of Illegitimate Needs

Illegitimate ego needs arise from feelings of self-doubt, shame, guilt, and worthlessness. If a person feels unworthy, helpless, and weak, he/she is likely to need to cling to and possess his/her mate. If he lacks self-trust, self-belief, and self-faith he will look toward the other to provide him with strength, succor, and feelings of esteem. A lack of self-confidence can lead one to attempt to maneuver the beloved into constantly bolstering one's self-image. Needless to say, the demand is insatiable and will eventually lead to feelings of disgust and resentment in the mate. Self-esteem implies self-acceptance.[14] Erich Fromm has persuasively contended that self-love is not to be confused with selfishness, or narcissistic egocentricity.[15] Most counselors and therapists make this contention in one way or another—that the person who lacks self-love will be a nonaccepting, selfish, selfless manipulator of others.[16]

Basically, however, illegitimate ego needs are the result of an actual love-security deficit or a perceived love-security deficit, which usually has resulted from being socialized by parents, teachers, and other authority figures bent on molding the child or teen-ager into a certain performance/behavior syndrome. The authority figures love the child but fall into the trap of withdrawing love, of failing to reassuringly demonstrate their esteem for the child as a person. Shaming and constant "putting down" may not seem very harmful or detrimental at the time, but in the long run such negative messages make a major contribution to the child's negative self-image. The child quickly learns patterns and methods of handling his emotions which form the groundwork for later neurotic tendencies. A vicious circle is set up in that any maladjustment or neurotic behavior on the part of the parents is bound to have consequences for the child who in turn will bring his negative self-image to his adulthood and thus his marriage and his children.

The need for accepting love and security needs in childhood have received empirical support from Harry F. Harlow, who demonstrated the importance of emotional warmth in the neonatal and infant phases of development in the rhesus monkey. Harlow designed a pair of surrogate mothers, one being a streamlined wire mother without a terry-cloth covering and the other with a terry-cloth covering. The monkeys, deprived of their natural mother, gravitated to the terry-cloth mother for very long periods of time and with greater frequency than to the non-terry-cloth mother, regardless of which mother "nursed" the neonate or infant. Harlow comments: "We were not surprised to discover that contact comfort was an important basic affectional or love variable, but we did not expect it to overshadow so completely the variable of nursing; indeed, the disparity is so great as to suggest that the primary function of nursing as an affectional variable is that of insuring frequent and intimate body contact of the infant with the mother. Certainly, man cannot live by milk alone. Love is an emotion that does not need to be bottle- or spoon-fed, and we may be sure that there is nothing to be gained by giving lip service to love." [17] Harlow's work has been a milestone in establishing the importance of contact comfort and the emotional security it facilitates in the infant monkey. It is probably not far afield to make a comparison with human infants and, if we do so, to realize that the theoretical work of clinicians such as Fromm, Horney, May, and Rogers is in sound empirical territory. A love deficit is, therefore, a deprivation either in infant contact comfort or a perception, due to later experience, that one was not loved. In either case, the deficit is a necessary and sufficient cause for what we have defined as illegitimate ego needs.

Illegitimate ego needs usually do not become apparent in nonintimate relationships. Persons sometimes reflect an amazing capacity to avoid deep interpersonal relationships even though they have no awareness of their own avoidance tactics or their need to protect themselves from being known by others. The greater majority of people do not avoid intimacy but disappointingly fail to achieve intimacy due to the intrusive negative effects of illegitimate ego needs learned in childhood. The greater the degree of closeness and intimacy, the more likely that illegitimate needs will take command of the personality, causing the individual to lay down impossible, unreasonable, and illogical demands and requests of the partner. These are the "nitty gritty" of resentment, irritability, and falling out of love.

B-Love and D-Love

Under the circumstances we have just considered, love can become confused with the partner's capacity to meet both legitimate and illegitimate ego needs. When an individual can unlearn his illegitimate ego needs (an admittedly slow, painful process), he is freer to express genuine love, which in its ideal state we call "B-love" or "being love." However, illegitimate ego-need fulfillment can give a person such a strong illusion of "security" (however temporary it may be) that the person mistakenly perceives fulfillment of his need as the essence of love. In truth it is "D-love" or "deficiency love." Maslow has contrasted B-love with D-love in a manner which illustrates the differences between legitimate and illegitimate ego needs. While B-love is entirely legitimate and D-love is entirely illegitimate, there is some mixture of both in most of us.

1. B-love is welcomed into consciousness, and is completely enjoyed. Since it is non-possessive, and is admiring rather than needing, it makes no trouble and is practically always pleasure-giving.

2. [B-love] can never be sated; it may be enjoyed without end. It usually grows greater rather than disappearing. It is intrinsically enjoyable. It is end rather than means.

3. The B-love experience is often described as being the same as, and having the same effects as, the aesthetic experience or the mystic experience.

4. The therapeutic and psychologic effects of experiencing B-love are very profound and widespread. Similar are the characterological effects of the relatively pure love of a healthy mother for her baby, or the perfect love of their God that some mystics have described.

5. B-love is, beyond the shadow of a doubt, a richer, "higher," more valuable subjective experience than D-love (which all B-lovers have also previously experienced). This preference is also reported by my other older, more average subjects, many of whom experience both kinds of love simultaneously in varying combinations.

6. D-love *can* be gratified. The concept "gratification" hardly applies at all to admiration-love for another person's admiration-worthiness and love-worthiness.

7. In B-love there is a minimum of anxiety-hostility. For all practical human purposes, it may even be considered to be absent. There *can,* of course, be anxiety-for-the-other. In D-love one must always expect some degree of anxiety-hostility.

8. B-lovers are more independent of each other, more autonomous, less jealous or threatened, less needful, more individual, more disinterested, but also simultaneously more eager to help the other toward self-actualization, more proud of his triumphs, more **altruistic,** generous and fostering.

Altruistic. Describing genuine concern for the welfare of others. Altruistic love is contrasted with egoistic love.

9. The truest, most penetrating perception of the other is made possible by B-love. It is as much a cognitive as an emotional-conative reaction . . .

10. Finally, I may say that B-love, in a profound but testable sense, creates the partner. It gives him a self-image, it gives him self-acceptance, a feeling of love worthiness, all of which permit him to grow. It is a real question whether the full development of the human being is possible without it.[18]

We began this chapter with a consideration of happiness. What do legitimate vs. illegitimate and B-love vs. D-love have to do with happiness? Answer: Everything. Happiness is a by-product of self-fulfillment and self-actualization. If a person is essentially an unhappy person, and he seeks happiness by marrying a person who promises to "make me happy," the prognosis is one of disillusionment, disappointment, and despair. He is, in effect, saying to his intended, "You must make me happy. You will be to me what no one has ever been to me. You will make up for all my previous unhappiness. You will make up for my own lack of fulfillment." As stated previously, no human being can rightfully expect another to bear such a burden for him. If, on the other hand, a person is essentially a happy person—that is, he has a reasonable amount of positive feelings of self-worth, self-acceptance, self-trust, and self-esteem—he may legitimately say, "I need you because I love you." "I anticipate a happy relationship as we grow together in caring, trusting, and being ourselves." Fromm has said that "love is an activity, not a passive affect; it is a 'standing in,' not a 'falling for.' In the most general way, the active character of love can be described by stating that love is primarily *giving*, not receiving. . . . Giving is the highest expression of potency. In the very act of giving, I experience my strength, my wealth, my power. This experience of heightened vitality and potency fills me with joy. I experience myself as overflowing, spending, alive, hence, as joyous. Giving is more joyous than receiving, not because it is a deprivation, but because in the act of giving lies the expression of my aliveness." [19]

We can say that the fulfillment of legitimate ego needs takes place in "B-love," which creates love by loving, and experiences happiness as the state of inward fulfillment that comes from the active loving of another person. Illegitimate ego needs find expression in "D-love," which needs to take love from the other in an attempt to achieve personal happiness. It isn't wrong to desire happiness in the marital relationship, but we can say with confidence that marital happiness lies *primarily* within oneself and *secondarily* in the other.

3 Sexuality and Value: An Existential Approach

Is there a void of meaning in today's culture? Can sex be termed only a pleasure orientation? Is hedonism a workable philosophy? Can sex be considered a value? Does sex exist in isolation from other values? Is pleasure a value in itself? Of what use is it to distinguish between intrinsic and extrinsic values? What are the conditions set up by a configuration of values? Can extramarital sex be a congruent value in a marital relationship? Under what conditions does extramarital sex destroy a configuration?

The Existential Concern

Sexual attitudes and behavior cannot be separated from the basic and ultimate questions of life. Indeed, in this age of anxiety the search for meaning and the need for affection, reassurance, security, and succor often masquerade as the sexual drive. Thus, the existential view of the search for meaning is useful to us if we are to understand the role of sexuality in our lives.

Existentialists focus on man's responsibility to define the meaning of his own existence. In Viktor Frankl's words, "The term 'existential' may be used in three ways: to refer to (1) *existence* itself, i.e., the specifically human mode of being; (2) the *meaning* of existence; and (3) the striving to find a concrete meaning in personal existence, that is, to say, the *will* to meaning." [1] For our purposes, we will focus on this third sense, the will to meaning. We shall adopt the existential stance that man is not born with an "essence" (that which makes him what he is); rather he exists first and is then faced with the challenge of endowing his life with meaning, purpose, value—essence. In placing existence before essence, existential philosophy goes against many traditions which consider man's true substance, his meaning, as a given, inextricably woven into the fabric of his being.

The existential *will to meaning* can be contrasted to the Freudian *pleasure principle* (will to seek pleasure and avoid pain) and the Adlerian concept of the *will to power*. Viktor Frankl made this distinction clear in his theory of logotherapy (*logos* is Greek for meaning):

> Logotherapy . . . focuses on the meaning of human existence as well as on man's search for such a meaning. According to logotherapy, the striving to find a meaning in one's life is the primary motivational force in man. . . . Logotherapy deviates from psychoanalysis insofar as it considers man as a being whose main concern consists in fulfilling a meaning and in actualizing values, rather than in the mere gratification and satisfaction of drives and instincts, the mere reconciliation of the conflicting claims of id, ego, and superego, or mere adaptation and adjustment to the society and environment.[2]

Other spokesmen for the general belief that man is responsible for himself and capable of creating his own meaning are philosophers Soren Kierkegaard, Martin Heidegger, Karl Jaspers, Hermann Hesse, Gabriel Marcel, and Paul Tillich, and psychologists Abraham Maslow, Rollo May, Erich Fromm, Everett Shostrom, Frederick Perls.

Man's search for meaning occurs in what Frankl refers to as an "existential vacuum." This vacuum in which man exists is characterized by meaninglessness, emptiness, nothingness, the dread of nonbeing, loneliness, and boredom, or *ennui*. It is man's task to confront this void and fabricate his own meaning.

Sex and Psychic Restlessness

It is nearly impossible to determine how much of today's sexual preoccupation and obsession is an attempt to overcome feelings of impotence in the face of the existential vacuum. However, it is apparent to psychologists, psychiatrists, and others that many people seem to seek out sexual activity in a manner that gives them little pleasure or joy. In line with this observation, it has been suggested that sex becomes a cover for various kinds of psychic distress and unrest. Karen Horney, for example, has suggested that "all is not sexuality that looks like it," indeed that sex is very often "an expression of the desire for reassurance" and that it is often "regarded as more a sedative than as genuine sexual enjoyment or happiness."[3]

Erich Fromm makes a similar point: "An insecure person who has an intense need to prove his worth to himself, to show others how irresistible he is, or to dominate others by 'making' them sexually, will easily feel intense sexual desires, and a painful tension if the desires are not satisfied."[4] However, as Fromm points out, these desires, while interpreted by the person as genuine physical needs, are merely stand-ins for less obvious psychic needs. A healthy sexuality is not based on such needs but rather is "rooted in abundance and freedom and is the expression of sensual and emotional productiveness." [5]

Another psychic need which is often repressed is the need to overcome the fear of death. Rollo May has made this point in his book *Love and Will*:

> What would we have to see if we could cut through our obsession about sex? That we must die. The clamor of sex all about us drowns out the ever-waiting presence of death . . . Death is the symbol of ultimate impotence and finiteness, and anxiety arising from this unescapable experience calls forth the struggle to make ourselves infinite by way of sex. Sexual activity is the most ready way to silence the inner dread of death, and through the symbol of procreation, to triumph over it . . . Repression of death equals obsession with sex. . . .[6]

Free-floating anxiety will readily attach itself to the sex drive in such a way that the subject is totally unaware of the inauthenticity of his sexual desire; his sexual preoccupation may be "acting out" behavior stemming from repression and suppression of his real ego needs. Frankl has remarked: ". . . there are various masks and guises under which the existential vacuum appears. Sometimes the frustrated will to meaning is vicariously compensated for by a will to power, including the most primitive form of the will to power, the will to money. In other cases, the place of frustrated will to meaning is taken by the will to pleasure. That is why existential frustration often eventuates in sexual compensation. We can observe, in such cases, that the sexual libido becomes rampant in the existential vacuum." [7] This sort of "rampant" sexual desire is illustrated by the following case study.

Case Study 3

Gary is in his early thirties, married, the father of one child, age 8. Gary was married once before; the marriage was of short duration and he has described it as simply two incompatible, immature people.

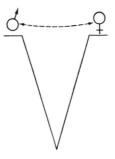

Figure 3-1
Sex and the Existential Void

Gary: I am here because I'm worried about myself. I feel tense and uptight most of the time; especially when I'm under any kind of pressure at work. My wife doesn't seem to understand and I sometimes feel resentful toward her. Several years ago I began to have sexual relations with a girl I had met at work. She was a lot of fun although I never really had any feelings for her . . . You'd have to understand that except for one or two occasional flings, I was pretty much on the up and up with my wife. I don't believe in extramarital sex but here I am—now I almost thrive on it. I go crazy for women. It's so easy—they are just asking for it . . . so why not? I don't think my wife knows it, although I'm sure she suspects things.

The trouble is I'm scared! I'm really worried that I'm abnormal. I feel like my sex drive is . . . well, you know . . . like I'm oversexed. I meet a girl and before you know it I'm in bed with her—sometimes I don't even know her name or what she looks like. All I know is that I gotta have her—my whole body vibrates with excitement and I act like I'm programmed to move right in! Then . . . well . . . then I feel better! Usually anyway . . . (pause). I've learned to ignore my conscience—hell, if I let my screwing bother me I'd die of guilt. Sometimes I do get depressed and down on myself . . . and then I make noble vows to myself . . . but . . . well, you know how long I stick to those. First chance I get—right back at it . . . I guess you could say I love it—but then I hate myself for loving it.

Gary is saying several things: He is bothered by his sexual appetite; he sometimes feels guilt, which bothers him, and at other times he successfully suppresses his guilt feelings; he wishes to be free of his compulsive behavior. Yet Gary may be saying something on a deeper level. He may be saying that he has an all-pervading disgust for himself, and he may be camouflaging his request for help in a request to help him curb his sexual appetite. As in all our case studies, the dynamics go far beyond our present illustrative purposes. However, it is safe to say that Gary's behavior is only a symptomatic indicator of an inner anxiety. Gary appears to be compulsively driven, and one can predict that he is highly indiscriminate in his choice of sexual partners. The case study reveals not only that "not all is sexual that looks sexual" but also a psychic inner conflict replete with anxiety, self-devaluation, and an absence of meaning and purpose. Under such conditions, we can see sex being used to fill the sensed existential vacuum.

Sexuality and the Question of Value

While Karen Horney uses the word sexuality it would have been more accurate if she had used "sex," "sexual," or "sexual activity." We shall reserve the word "sexuality" for the total fusion of sex with personal identity, for human sexuality includes the entire sexual identity and psychic orientation of the human individual; it is part of and dependent upon one's self-concept. The terms *masculinity* and *femininity* similarly describe more than just male and female. They are psychological constructs relating one's sexual identity to the whole of one's personality structure. When we say that someone lacks confidence about their masculinity or femininity, we are not simply speaking of male or female genitalia. Rather, we are asking a question about identity and how one relates oneself to the essential core of one's being. Sexuality is bound up with the sense of self—self-esteem, self-acceptance, self-regard, self-confidence, and self-trust.

The relationship between the existential vacuum and human sexual behavior is, indeed, valid in that man is never an isolated sexual creature, nor is he an isolated organism set apart from the milieu in which he lives, breathes, works, suffers, and enjoys. He is subject to great issues and nagging trivia. Foreign policy, national policy, population crises, ecology concerns, poverty, law and order, revolutionary movements and questions of personal and social ethics are problems that thrust themselves upon man. Yet this only seems to increase our sense of frustration at our human weakness and impotency as we look at these issues as individual citizens. Large-scale government, corporations, business, rising cost of food and shelter, and an all-enveloping political bureaucracy can dwarf man's individual capacity for effecting change and cause him great frustration and feelings of impotence. A person can fall into an apathetic stance as he ponders what he can do as an individual. People start asking themselves "What can one person do?"

Compounding the problem is the changing complexion of our religious-ecclesiastical credo. Some will deny that we are living in the "post-Christian" era. Nevertheless there has been a turning away from the traditional Christian ethos and dogma as reflected by those of the theological establishment who seek to go beyond a belief in a personalized God to a more general belief in a dynamic creating force (cosmic ultimacy). Many things are implied in the phrase, "the death of God," but implicit in most of them is the belief that no longer can man look to a posited deity to provide an escape from the realities of human existence. Paul Tillich had expressed this thought long before the radical theologians picked up Nietzsche's idea concerning the death of God. Tillich characterizes our present age as the age of spiritual anxiety in that man is threatened by an all-pervading sense of emptiness and meaninglessness. "The distinction of the three types of anxiety is supported by the history of Western civilization. We find that at the end of ancient civilization **ontic anxiety** is predominant, at the end of the Middle Ages **moral anxiety,** and at the end of the modern period **spiritual anxiety.** But in spite of the predominance of one type the others are also present and effective." [8] Man's ontic self-affirmation comes is threatened by fate and death; his moral self-affirmation is threatened by guilt and condemnation; and the threat to his spiritual self-affirmation comes in the form of emptiness and meaninglessness.

It is significant that the three main periods of anxiety appear at the end of an era. The anxiety which, in its different forms, is potentially present in every individual becomes general if the accustomed structures of meaning, power, belief, and order disintegrate. These structures, as long as they are in force, keep anxiety bound within a

---

Ontic anxiety. Anxiety arising from man's fear of the unknown and the reality of death or nonbeing.

Moral anxiety. In Tillich's sense, anxiety arising from man's concern with punishment and guilt for sin. More generally, anxiety caused by a conflict between values.

Spiritual anxiety. Emptiness and despair arising from a threat to traditional spiritual values or a threat of loss of meaning and purpose.

protective system of courage by participation. The individual who participates in the institutions and ways of life of such a system is not liberated from his personal anxieties but he has means of overcoming them with well-known methods. In periods of great changes these methods no longer work.[9]

⸲h maintains that because we are living in a period of great ⸱ᴬditional means of coping with anxiety no longer work. ⸲ymbols no longer convey the meaning which they did ⸲erations. Ancient formulas and creedal statements are elevant to modern man, not because they are wrong but ₅ey cannot be understood today in any meaningful way. As ₅ays, "It can be the fact that they are no longer understood in original power of expressing the human situation and of anᵣ₎ring existential human questions. This is largely the case with the ₀octrinal symbols of Christianity." [10] Thus, according to Tillich, only the "courage to be," which implies a participation in the "power of being itself," can enable man to take on his own ontic insecurity, his spiritual incertitude, and his moral imperfection. Man is threatened by nonbeing. The "courage to be" is the courage to take the anxiety of nonbeing unto oneself. *Neurotic anxiety,* is the inability to take one's existential anxiety upon oneself. "Neurotic anxiety builds a narrow castle of certitude which can be defended and is defended with the utmost tenacity. Man's power of asking is prevented from becoming actual in this sphere, and if there is a danger of its becoming actualized by questions asked from the outside he reacts with a fanatical rejection." [11]

The existential dilemma today is due to a breakdown of traditional systems which formerly served to protect man from his anxiety. The challenge is to test our capacity to define for ourselves the meaning and values by which we desire to live.

Ontic and spiritual self-affirmation must be distinguished but they cannot be separated. Man's being includes his relation to meanings. He is human only by understanding and shaping reality, both his world and himself, according to meanings and values. His being is spiritual even in the most primitive expressions of the most primitive human being . . . Therefore the threat to his spiritual being is a threat to his whole being. The most revealing expression of this fact is the desire to throw away one's ontic existence rather than stand the despair of emptiness and meaninglessness. The death instinct is not an ontic but a spiritual phenomenon. Freud identified this reaction to the meaninglessness of the never-ceasing, and never-satisfied libido with man's essential nature. But it is only an expression of his existential self-estrangement and of the disintegration of his spiritual life into meaninglessness.[12]

One way of escaping from the challenge to create value and meaning is to embrace hedonism, or the will to pleasure. For some, this solution will work. For others, it will only work superficially to assuage the repressed restlessness that gnaws away like a termite. Thus, hedonism probably becomes a pseudoescape for many people, resulting only in redoubled attempts to obtain pleasure when the spectre of emptiness raises its ugly head. Is this not the state of much hedonistic preoccupation today? Is it not true that we have experienced, in a deep and profound sense, a loss of meaning and value? Failing to make sense of this "loss," we have opted for a shallow hedonism or we have repressed our existential doubts in order to remain faithful to the traditional symbols, creeds, and dogmas within the traditions of Western thought. Some have opted for Eastern thought, but here too is a dilemma, since the Western mind is socialized in a Western pattern and cannot readily internalize Eastern paradoxes.

Liberation from the narrow antisensual and antisexual bonds of Victorianism and Puritanism is indeed something of value. Who among us would wish for the return of a rigidly repressed sexual orientation? In vain these traditions have protested that sex is good, only to have the message contradicted by warnings, limits, preachments and hortatory which effectively served to give a metacommunication, a message about the message. Sex is good and to be enjoyed but be careful, because it is also dirty and essentially enjoyable only to the lower instincts of the human self. As Rollo May says, "In Victorian times, when the denial of sexual impulses, feelings and drives was the mode and one would not talk about sex in polite company, an aura of sanctifying repulsiveness surrounded the whole topic. Males and females dealt with each other as though neither possessed sexual organs." [13]

The question is raised: What, then, is wrong with hedonism? Agreement about an answer will be difficult to attain, but I would suggest that a moment-to-moment pleasure orientation fails to satisfy man's quest for fulfillment. Many, undeniably, who go the hedonistic route sing forth its praises. Others attempt to go the hedonistic road and valiantly persevere only to confess that their inner state is no better than it was.

Case Study 4

A college senior writes: "To the amazement of my friends, I am honestly able to pick up the phone at any time and get a bed partner. I can even vary the bed partners as I have more than one. This sounds so smug on my part, yet I say it in amazement. I have sought sex as an avenue to status and find it empty. Do not misunderstand me; sex, even without passion, has its rewards. Yet those rewards are no longer enough. Sex has proved to be a momentary passionless thing. It has become rewarding only in the short-run. At times, I find myself using it as a sleeping aid! . . . Here I am. I am dissatisfied with passionless sex and dissatisfied with a relationship devoid of sex. I seem unable to find both in a single person. I am looking for the total communication that will make someone unique to me and me unique to that person. I seek to have a great value placed on my existence, and to place an equally great value on that person's existence. I hope to raise a family. I want to experience what must be the unique joy of realizing that this communication of two people has created a third individual; different from both, yet the product of both."

We reject hedonism as a viable way to fill the existential void or as a way to compensate for not being otherwise able to fill it. With equal conviction we reject the nonsexual, antisexual, repressed-sexual stance of Victorianism, Puritanism, postreformation, and postcounterreformation theology.

Yet another dilemma presses upon us. If we wish to avoid the antisexual emphasis of Victorianism and reject hedonism, what is left? What would a synthesis entail? How can man fulfill his quest for meaning and value as well as his desire for pleasure, enjoyment, and fun? What would a synthesis reject from these polar approaches to sexuality? The rejection should probably take the form of refusing to accept exclusively the essential tenet of each tradition: that sex is only pleasure and that sex is an uninvited guest into the household of the human organism.

A synthesis should probably start with looking at the idea that pleasure is or has the potential to be a value in itself—not merely as a means to some other end but as an end in itself. Pleasure is its own reward. It does not need to be rationalized, nor does it need justification to make it worthwhile. Pleasure does not benefit from an authoritarian tradition that does not allow people to be rid of guilt when they enjoy themselves. Human experience would seem to indicate that pleasure has always been valued for its own sake, regardless of philosophical, theological, and moralistic reservations about the dangers of hedonism. Yet we have actually been conditioned in a kind of reverse reasoning process that finds pleasure in the violation of rules rather than in the observance of enjoyment. Thus, the price one pays is guilt; guilt becomes sole witness to the desirability of pleasure.

The greater the taboo against pleasure, the greater the possibility of guilt if the taboo is violated. The taboo against masturbation serves to trigger guilt even in those who only daydream or fantasize about it, even though they resist the act itself. If the guilt outweighs the pleasure, then one concludes that the pleasure wasn't worth the price. If the pleasure wins out over the guilt, then one would logically conclude that mental pain (guilt) was less than the rewarding pleasure. One need not confine oneself to sex in illustrating the value of pleasure. Prohibitions against lipstick, hair-dos, dancing, movies, television, eating, and drinking abundantly illustrate some of the traditional fears of pleasure. According to some moralists, if man is a creature with a higher, godly nature and a lower, demonic nature, then those things which feed the desires of the lower nature need to be discouraged. Yet man has always succeeded in flirting with pleasure despite the threat of punishment or guilt. The dilemma can only be resolved by rejecting an ethic which claims that pleasure is wrong or evil and proceeding to find a fulfilling role for pleasure to play in our revised value system.

Nevertheless, if pleasure is intrinsically valuable, does this imply that the value of sexual relations is only or exclusively in the sexual act itself? I think not. A clear distinction should be made between intrinsic and extrinsic values. An intrinsic value is inherent to the object that is valued. Intrinsic valuation is philosophically considered to be *objective* in that the value resides in the object itself. An extrinsic value is external to the object and lies in the attitude or mind of the person doing the valuing. Thus, it is philosophically considered a *subjective* value. (Beauty is in the eye of the beholder; ugliness is in the eye of the beholder.) I would like to contend for the position that sexual relations are intrinsically meaningful because they are pleasurable, not simply because someone has specified the conditions under which they are allowed to be meaningful. Nevertheless, when sexual relations are **congruent** with other values, a **configuration** of value is formed which is extrinsic to the sexual relationship itself but serves thereby to enrich the sexual relationship so that it can be both intrinsically and extrinsically meaningful.

Congruency and Configuration

We can say that pleasure is its own value and therefore is its own meaning, but we should also point out that life is not fulfilled when its meaning is confined to one type of experience, in this case the pleasurable experience. Fulfillment is a configuration of values, each different, yet each congruent with the others.

If a value is devoid of meaning, then one would hardly be justified in calling that value pleasurable, because pleasure itself can be meaningful. One may ask in all seriousness if something can be of value if it is not pleasurable. Suffering is not usually pleasurable, but it can have meaning. Bereavement at the loss of a loved one is not pleasurable, but the experience is meaningful precisely because of a prior existing meaningful relationship. Death is a meaningful experience, even though it is painful and nonpleasurable. Indeed, is it not true that as we contemplate our own nonbeing, it gives new meaning and importance to our being? Life as we know it on this planet has a beginning and an end. If we knew that we would never die, would the events in our lives have as much meaning for us?

The existential challenge, by its very nature, is a challenge which each person must meet alone. No one person can ever define or fulfill the meaning of another person's existence. Unfortunately, some try. Unfulfilled parents will look to their children to fulfill their own lack of fulfillment. Husbands will look to wives and wives to husbands. Children, too, will sometimes yearn to remain emotionally dependent upon their parents, inwardly wanting the parents to help them give their lives meaning and purpose. Parents can give direction, guidance, and a framework for determining values, but they cannot define or fulfill the meaning and intrinsic value of their child's life.

Congruent. Describing an agreement, conformity, or correspondence of two or more factors such that there is a minimum of disparity or conflict. Harmonious.

Configuration. An arrangement of parts to create a forming together and blending together without conflict. In psychology, a configuration is often termed a *gestalt.*

The establishment of meaning is also thwarted if one attempts to stick with only one value orientation. When meaning is restricted to one kind of value it becomes narrowed down, constricted, and therefore neurotic. This is the fallacy of hedonism, which focuses solely on the value of pleasure. Similarly, to restrict one's definition of man to so-called higher nature or lower nature is a constriction which dehumanizes him.

Eastern thought teaches us a great deal about paradoxical logic, whereas Western thought has somewhat rigidly followed the cause and effect of Aristotelian logic. Paradoxical logic teaches us that there would be no cold if there were no hot; there would be no joy if there were no sorrow or pain; there would be no good if there were no bad; there would be no love if there were no hate and anger; there would be no faith if there were no doubt; there would be no passion if there were no stoic dispassion; there could be no security if there were no anxiety; there would be no possibility of "being" if there were no possibility of "nonbeing"; there would be no meaning if there were no possibility of meaninglessness; and there would be no value if there were no possibility of worthlessness.

When values, however paradoxical they may be, form a configuration and when they are congruent with each other life takes on its own meaning in the sense that the meaning of human existence is intrinsic to the very process of living. When values are congruent they may be quite different and include a wide range of possibilities, but they are not in conflict. They are compatible, they fit in with each other, thus forming a configuration that consists of many parts. A true configuration of values allows for human diversity, spontaneity, and growth. Thus, the meaning that one chooses to give to his own existence is greater than the sum of the several parts, because these parts interact, complement, and otherwise feed into each other, forming a holistic pattern.

Sex is such a value; it exists as part of a meaningful configuration. Sex, sexuality, and sensuousness are values, not in isolation, but in relation to each other and to the whole. Similarly, pleasure is a value that must be congruent with other values within the configuration. Let us consider as illustration the various possible sexual responses, attitudes, and desires of married people. One couple's configuration could conceivably consist of valuing sex as fun and intrinsically enjoyable, with a great value placed on such other factors as fidelity to one's mate, interpersonal trust, firm commitment, the feeling of love as embodied in acts of caring, sharing, and facing conflict. The configuration may or may not include children, with or without certain shared assumptions about how the children are to be cared for and socialized. All of these parts may be intrinsically valuable, but a greater (extrinsic) meaning comes from the fact that the values are congruent and work with each other in the total configuration.

Another couple's configuration might represent sex as intrinsically valuable but consider freedom more valuable than fidelity or monogamous exclusiveness. Whether or not these values are congruent would depend on such factors as whether both spouses held these beliefs or whether one spouse held different values. For example, it would hardly be congruent for a husband to embrace freedom in sexual contacts for himself and deny equal freedom to his wife.

Figure 3–2 might represent the value configuration of our first couple, with one noncongruent value damaging the configuration. The noncongruency of a single value can be necessary and sufficient cause to put the configuration into disharmony and dysfunction.

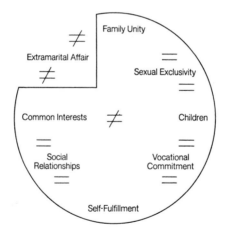

Figure 3–2
A Broken Configuration—One Noncongruent Value

Figure 3–2 also reflects the situation portrayed in the following case study.

Case Study 5

Mike and Sally are in their middle forties. Mike is an engineer in a small industry. Mike and Sally have been married for 24 years, with neither having been previously married. They have four children, ranging in age from 16 to 22. Mike and Sally are in conjoint marital counseling.

Sally: "I've thought a long time about what I'd say to you (the counselor) when I first came to you—but now that we're here I don't know how to begin . . . It all seems so jumbled . . . like . . . like the bottom has fallen out of our marriage. We were so happy—at least I thought so—but now this! I knew Mike was restless but I never dreamed he would actually . . . actually . . . (pause). How could he do this to me. We've had arguments and differences, sure—but nothing to cause any serious barrier between us. Just the other day I was talking long distance to my sister and I was telling her how Mike and I valued all the different things we enjoy in life—the kids, our home, our interests—but now . . . Oh how can I ever face her after saying that. I guess I'm more angry and hurt than I am jealous. I trusted him. He always seemed to enjoy sex with me. He teased me once in a while—but I enjoyed intercourse . . .

Mike: I think you're overdoing this, Sally! Look, I'm not leaving you or anything like that. I told you I was sorry. We do have a lot going for us—do you honestly think I don't care about you or the kids?

Sally: How could you?

Mike: I told you I was sorry. What more is there to say? It was just a physical thing. I don't have any feelings for her.

Sally: God, don't tell me that—it just makes the whole thing worse.

The dynamics in this broken configuration are many and varied, and include suppressed conflict and repressed anger. Nevertheless, there is no reason the preexisting configuration cannot be restored. When a relationship is defined as being built on mutual trust, there can be no painless way to deal with the consequences of broken trust. If Mike were pressed he would probably not deny that the extramarital experience was indeed pleasurable. In this particular marriage, however, Mike's activity has created a rupture in a meaningful configuration. In our terminology, intrinsic pleasure with a third person has temporarily destroyed the extrinsic meaning and value of the sexual relationship within the marital dyad.

Figure 3–3 represents a life situation in which all of the values are congruent. The total congruency eliminates severe strain or conflict and allows a configuration of value to be formed that is extrinsic to every one of the individual values but which, nevertheless, gives an added meaning to each of the individual values beyond their intrinsic value.

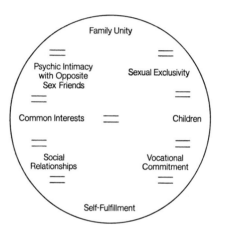

Figure 3–3
A Configuration of Congruent Values

Figure 3–4 represents another life situation in which all of the values are congruent. While the values are contrary to those of the previous illustration, they are, nevertheless, congruent because they are not in conflict and are jointly held, thus protecting the configuration.

The reader will note that whether or not an extramarital relationship will rupture a meaningful configuration depends on the perceived value of the sexual relationship and the agreed-upon definition of the marital relationship. (See Chapter 6 for further discussion of permissive monogamy.)

The thrust of this chapter is that sex is often used as a means of warding off anxiety and filling the emptiness of the existential vacuum. This orientation often proves to be self-defeating in that the value of sexual pleasure is considered in isolation and is not related to other meaningful constructs in one's life. We have stressed that sex is

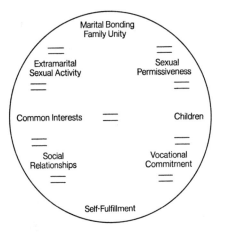

Figure 3–4
A Configuration in which
Extramarital Permissiveness Is a Congruent Value

indeed "meaningful pleasure" but that when this particular meaning-ful pleasure is in congruence with other values and other meaningful constructs a configuration of meaning is formed that is not only much greater than the sum of its parts but is the essence of a meaningful existence.

Sexual expression is pleasurable and as such is a value. Whether or not this value is congruent with other values will determine whether or not there will be a configuration. Individual values may have intrinsic meaning, but if the values are congruent there is the added possibility of the extrinsic value provided by a configuration. The existential vacuum is an expression of loss of value and loss of congruence in value; and hence, the lack of any meaningful configuration.

If interpersonal fusion—a deep feeling of oneness and unity—is considered to be something of value, then not only will coitus and sexual expression provide meaningful physical and psychic pleasure, but it will also make possible the pleasure of achieving an intimacy and a oneness—an aesthetic pleasure of extrinsic value.

4　Romance, Sex, and Marriage: An Unlikely Triad

What is implied by the term "romantic?" What role does romance play in sex and marriage? Do romance, sex, and marriage have to be incompatible? What is the alternative to romantic love? What is love? Of what use are the three kinds of love described by the Greeks—philos, eros, agape? Has our culture become confused in its approach to love and sex? What makes for a thriving marital configuration?

Romance: Two Points of View

The romantic movement of modern times is an outgrowth of the courtly tradition of the twelfth century. Hugo Beigel has delineated three periods during which ideals of courtly love have surfaced. These ideals originated in the twelfth century, surfaced again in the nineteenth century, and are now present in modern love, which he sees as ". . . a derivative, modified in concord with the conditions of our age and based more on ego demands than on ideal demands." [1] Thus, romanticism has always been changing as it is adapted to the needs of a particular age. Beigel characterizes courtly love as

> *l'amour de lohh* (distant love), or *minne,* and many documents, poems, and epics depict its form and the feelings involved. . . . Courtly love was the conventionalization of a new ideal that arose in the feudal class and institutionalized certain aspects of the male-female relationship *outside marriage.* In conformity with the Christian concept of and contempt for sex, the presupposition for *minne* was chastity. Being the spiritualization and sublimation of carnal desire, such love was deemed to be impossible between husband and wife. By application of the religious concept of abstract love to the "mistress," the married woman of the ruling class who had lost her economic function, was endowed with higher and more general values: gentleness and refinement. Unselfish service to the noble lady became a duty of the knight, explicitly sworn to the oath the young nobleman had to take at the dubbing ceremony. [2]

53

Not until the second phase, more often known as the Romantic movement, did sexual expression become explicitly acceptable: "Under the increasing discomfort in a changing civilization, the aristocratic class had found a way to alleviate the defeats of a family-prescribed monogamous marriage by dividing duty and satisfaction; the woman reserved her loyalty for her husband and her love for her gallant. Continuing on the tracks laid by the concept of courtly love, the nobles of the seventeenth and eighteenth centuries in Austria, Spain, France, and the Netherlands, etc. still adhered to the tenet that love and marriage were irreconcilable." [3] However, sex and love were well integrated, if only outside marriage.

The modern stage aims at the integration of love and marriage. "No longer was there to be a cleavage between the spirituality of love and the marital sex relation; but the latter was sanctified by the former." [4] This type of love became a hallmark of the literary and operatic works in the romantic tradition. Hence, in these three stages we see: (1) love outside marriage but basically without sex, (2) love outside marriage with sex, and (3) love and sex united within marriage. Such generalizations are, of course, oversimplified, and exceptions to each period's ideals were legion. Nevertheless, note the trend of drawing sex and love into an adulterous union and then into a legal union. Note also that the chief symbol of romanticism seems to be an idealized woman who is an object of veneration and adoration with or without sexual relations.

Albert Ellis gives a somewhat different account of the growth of romanticism. Whereas Beigel assesses the Romantic movement as a necessary antidote to social breakdown and feelings of helplessness, Ellis does not see redeeming features in romanticism. To Ellis, romanticism is an "idealized, perfectionist emotion" that "thrives on intermittent rather than steady association between two lovers." [5] Contrary to popular assumptions, romantic love does not necessarily thrive on increased sexual expression or on offspring, nor is it guaranteed to survive the lover's aging process. "Consequently, the utter, terrible disillusionment of many or most romantic lovers becomes eventually assured . . . the romantic lover exaggerates, overestimates, sees his beloved as she really is not . . . when their expectations are ultra-romantic, and hence unrealistic, failure to achieve their level of aspiration must inevitably ensue: with consequent unhappiness and a tendency toward emotional disturbance." [6] Ellis sees romanticism as essentially antisexual, for sex is employed only as a means of attracting and holding the male.

> The pattern of courtship in America and in practically all of Western civilized society is that of the Sex Tease. In following this pattern, the modern woman, whether she consciously knows it or not, is forcibly striving to do two major things: First, to make herself appear infinitely sexually desirable—but finally approachable only in legal marriage. Second, to use sex as a bait and therefore to set it up as something special. If she gives in too easily to sex pleasure, she loses her favorite man-conquering weapon. Hence she must retain sexuality on a special plane, and dole it out only under unusual conditions. . . . Where romance is the rule, sex is virtually never enjoyed for itself. It is invariably hemmed in by idealistic, non-practical love restrictions. Romanticism, hand in hand with the sex tease game of American courtship, often plays up the verbal and plays down the active expression of human sexuality.[7]

Ellis faults romanticism chiefly on these two counts: creating unrealistic expectations and using sex as a lure, hence as a means to an end rather than as an end in itself. Beigel, writing from a sociohistorical point of view, holds to the alternate thesis that courtly love and romantic love are expressions of a process of reconciliation between human needs and frustrating sociocultural conditions. Beigel feels that romanticism has been scapegoated unfairly as being the villain in present-day marital disillusionment: Ellis, on the other hand, thinks that romanticism is one of the chief villains.

Current Trends

It is obvious today that the modern derivative of romanticism takes the form of a societal emphasis on certain aspects of the historical reality. A survey of television commercials, movie magazines, confessional magazines, television shows, advertising, and popular songs leads one to conclude that romantic love and sex are highly marketable commodities.[8] Deodorants, hair sprays, cosmetics, shaving lotions, and perfumes are multibillion-dollar sellers, sold by the lure of sexiness. If the population of the United States is coming of age in matters of sexual attitude, it is not discernible in American advertising and marketing procedures. In advertising, aimed not only at the unmarried but increasingly at the married as well, the lure of romance is virtually inseparable from sex. Sex is packaged as the ticket to romance; the romantic illusion is, in fact, the acceptable cultural "cover" for selling sex. One suspects that this implication—romance justifies the sexual—makes it possible for the general populace to accept sexual connotations. Without the romantic motif, we would be face to face with sex for its own sake. Perhaps this would be more honest but, as Madison Avenue knows quite well, it would not sell. The citizens of this country do not yet seem to take kindly to the straightforward approach.

X-rated movies portraying adults engaged in various sexual acts, suggest the frank embracing of physical sexual pleasure without any reference to love, commitment, value, or meaning. The success of some of these movies is an indication that increasing numbers within our population can accept sexual activity devoid of any romantic or other rationalizations; to this extent, this attitude may be considered honest. I would guess that this type of sexual stimuli will always be accessible but that after the stimuli have endured one or two generations a great amount of it will fall by the wayside. Slowly but surely the American citizen will learn to live with sexual frankness and interpersonal sexual honesty. However, what has been culturally repressed for several centuries is not likely to get unrepressed without an intermediate overreaction.

There is a dilemma to be found here. The mass media use romantic allusions in order to justify the sexual, yet when the sexual stands on its own—as in pornography, "adult literature," and X-rated films—there seems to be an existential emptiness. It appears that as a culture, we either avoid embracing sex by disguising it under the "rubric" of romanticism or we go 180 degrees in the opposite direction and embrace it in its most extreme expressions.

Rollo May has said that puritanism is based on love without sex but that today's "neopuritanism" wants sex without love.

> In our new puritanism, bad health is equated with sin. Sin used to mean giving in to one's sexual desires; it now means not having full sexual expression. Our contemporary puritan holds that it is immoral *not* to express your libido. . . . This all means, of course, that people not only have to learn to perform sexually but have to make sure, at the same time, that they can do so without letting themselves go in passion or unseemly commitment—the latter of which may be

interpreted as exerting an unhealthy demand upon the partner. *The Victorian person sought to have love without falling into sex; the modern person seeks to have sex without falling into love.*[9]

The problem still remains: Sex and love are reconciled in puritanism by the denial of sex, and in neopuritanism by the denial of love. The sexual reductionists want sex for its own sake devoid of all extraneous feelings, values, meanings, and sentiments, while the romanticists use romance as the rubric under which sex is legitimate, whether within or without marriage. In neither tradition does one find any reference to a single permissive standard such as "permissiveness with affection." [10] The problem, however, is not simply to arrive at a consensus on a single sexual standard to replace abstinence or the double standard. The challenge is to combine a "sexual" standard with an "affect" standard in order to make possible an integrated, viable union of two people over time. This, then, is our central question: can sex, love, and marriage be combined into an enduring relationship that will not compromise authenticity? Is there an alternative to the modern derivative of romantic love that will not do violence to sex, love, or marriage? One could wish for an easy answer, but the history of marital customs, love relationships, and sexual expression precludes any possibility of an easy solution.[11]

The Death of Romanticism

If romanticism were dead would we be any poorer? Ellis thinks not. Beigel seems to feel that we would. Beigel concludes that young people must be aided "in the discrimination of those qualities in themselves and the prospective mate which must balance each other to ensure the satisfaction of emotional, sexual, and personality needs and, in so doing, the greater durability of their union." [12] While Beigel treats romanticism quite fairly in his attempt to show how it has been falsely maligned, he nevertheless concludes by stating that the solution must be a balance between emotional, sexual, and personality needs.

Perhaps the kindest thing our society could do with its *romanticism* is to give it the dignity of a decent burial. In order for something to be born, there is often something which must first die. Romanticism has bequeathed to us much that is good, as Ellis points out, but it has, in the process, been directly and indirectly responsible for unrealistic expectations about emotional satisfaction in marriage, sexual satisfaction, and the raising of children. The role of conflict between spouses, the facing of anger, resentment, disappointment, sadness, tragedy, crises of all kinds, and the possibilities of self-fulfillment and self-actualization are precluded by a romantic frame of reference. The following hypothetical question-response dialogue may be helpful in understanding the need for a way of relating other than romanticism.

Question: Is there no place left for romance?

Response: No, if by "romance" one means romanticism as a tradition; however, there is another kind of romance that places value on affection, commitment, trust, and tenderness. If this kind of romance is added to open confrontation of one's feelings, an honest handling of conflict, a mutual desire to explore sexual needs, desires, and preferences, the forthright acceptance of responsibility for oneself, acceptance of the challenge of change and personal growth, self-fulfillment and self-actualizing experiences, freedom to be oneself and to avoid manipulative techniques in relating to the other, then there is a basis for keeping "romance" in marriage.

Question: Then why use the word "romance" at all? Aren't you talking about love?

Response: Yes, of course, but it's not necessarily the same as traditional "romantic love."

Question: How is it different?

Response: The kind of love I am referring to is not for romanticists. Romantic love idealizes the love object. Romantic love does not allow for the creative facing of conflict; rather it avoids conflict. Romantic love thrives in an atmosphere of high-pitched emotionality. Romantic love necessarily does not permit the lovers to be constantly together, else the emotionality would be reduced. The kind of love I'm talking about accepts the realities of real human relationships and thus makes possible a deeper, more fulfilling intimacy than that made possible by traditional romantic love.

The common expression "the honeymoon is over" is an interesting commentary on people's dependence on the concept of romantic love. Lovers who are courting have a distance between them that tends to color and heighten their interaction when they come together. The honeymoon places them together for a continuous period of time during which they can simply enjoy each other. The experience may prove to be disillusioning, however, in that once they have the freedom to enjoy their relationship they discover that there is now less emotionality since they know there is no approaching separation. When conflict of any kind enters the relationship, there is a threatening, foreboding awareness that the union lacks perfection and that the man and woman are fallible human beings after all. The discovery, often disillusioning and disappointing, that the feverish romantic pitch of idealistic oneness and enchantment cannot be sustained on a day-in, day-out basis gives birth to such resigned, antiromantic expressions as "the honeymoon is over."

Case Study 6

Hal and Jayne have been married five months. Jayne has felt increasing degrees of loneliness, unhappiness, and depression.

Jayne: I guess we aren't compatible. I just feel . . . well, like it's all over between us. Before we were married everything was great. We had FUN together! Now . . . well . . . now we just seem to abide each other. Honestly, I don't see how a person could change so quickly. Hal used to be fun! I mean really groovy. But now it's work, work, work! Weekends are even a bore. At least we have a few friends. It's like we—would you believe it—like we don't have anything to say to each other any more. I thought I could make Hal happy. He's happier than I am—that's for sure. He seems content to work all day and then sit and read the paper when he gets home. He's a golf nut. . . . I thought marriage was going to be exciting and fun—Wow! He used to tease me and do things to turn me on—now I feel like all he really wants is sex. We had sex before marriage and it was great. I felt loved and . . . like I was really a part of him. We were one. Now we just seem to go through the motions.

Hal: I guess you could say that things have changed. I love Jayne, but (pause . . . and another pause) it's just that I can't seem to do anything to make her happy or perk her up! Of course things aren't dashing and exciting anymore. Look—I enjoy doing the same things now that I did before we were married only now instead of picking her up and going out we begin and end at the same place! How could that change everything? . . . But it does! I work all day and when I get home it's almost like I'm supposed to become a different person and court her all evening long. Sex is different too—but to me it's just as much fun as ever—it's only that now I don't spend two or three hours wining and dining her every time we have intercourse. Look—I can't! We don't have that much dough and I've got a lot of other things that demand my time—my boss isn't the most patient guy in the world, you know . . . What gets me is I never thought Jayne would be like this after we were married. She used to be—well, everything I did was OK with her. Now we're married. Big deal.

Of course the honeymoon is over. The assumption that a relationship will remain the same when its terms are changed so drastically can only be an assumption born of unrealistic expectations. Jayne and Hal probably have a great deal going for them, but they might prematurely separate never having given themselves the opportunity to work through their differences, especially Jayne's disillusionment. One might explore Hal and Jayne's role expectations as husband and wife. One might be interested to know more about their personal history and their method of handling conflict during their engagement period. At a minimum, however, we can see that we have a carry-over of romantic expectations which now cause the pain of disappointment. The mystique created by distance and time is now erased by a common living arrangement. The honeymoon *is* over, and married life is de-idolized. The crisis that Jayne and Hal face will probably be the making or breaking point in their marriage inasmuch as crises of this kind can lead to insight, understanding, and growth provided the two are mutually able to work through some of their fantastic and unrealistic premarital expectations and to redefine their life together so as to create vitality and variety in sex, love, and daily interaction.

Question: Then what kind of love can survive marriage?
Response: Certainly not the romantic type of love which we've been discussing. Some call nonromantic married love "conjugal love" or "familial love." Others describe the relationship as "companionate marriage," "colleague marriage," or "partner marriage."
These terms may be helpful in describing a marriage between equals who define their own goals and values. Nevertheless, such a marriage is sustained not by romantic love but a mixture of sexual, erotic, philial, and agape love.

Sex, Eros, Philos, Agape

The English language is truly impoverished when it comes to the usage and meaning of the word "love." Love refers to anything from soup to nuts, including football, movies, foods, cars, fashions, experiences and feelings. We have often heard people say:

I love football.
I love mini-skirts.
I love romantic movies.
I love to ski.
I love martinis and roast beef.

Marital love, conjugal love, companionate love, infatuation, puppy love, sexual love, parent love, friendship love, patriotic devotion, and religious devotion all lean heavily on the word "love." Even bumper stickers on cars suggest that if you don't love America you'd better leave it. The unspoken premise is, of course, that if one truly loves America one would never criticize it or find fault with it. This narrow concept of love is an example of how words can convey different things to different people. I, for example, will stay in the United States because I love my native land and, therefore, in a given situation I will criticize, dissent, protest, vote, run for office, make political enemies, demonstrate, boycott—all of this *because* I love!

"Love" is also used to refer to sexual activity. To "make love" is commonly understood as referring to coitus and sexual play.

The ancient Greeks used three words for love. *Philos* referred to friendship, the kind of love between equals. Philos comes down to us as brotherly love (hence the word "Philadelphia," the city of brotherly love). A second Greek word, *eros,* describes the physical love between a man and a woman. Eros is the drive to create, to procreate, to communicate to another person in the most intimate way possible. *Agape* is the prototype of the unconditional, pure kind of love which, in its theological form, represents love of a deity for man. Agape is unearned, unmerited, unconditional, and undeserved. Agape says, "I love you in spite of" rather than "because of." This is the kind of love parents have for their children, although in a less ideal state. "We love you in spite of the trouble you have gotten into," rather than "We love you because you are such a good boy." In the marital relationship, agape love implies an acceptance of the mate as a fallible human being without implicit conditions or demands to change or to conform to the other's image.

Rollo May points out that in Western tradition we have used sex, lust, or libido to replace eros, which combines physical and psychic intimacy. He suggests that we have detached sexual love from erotic love and left little passion or creativity in sex.

> My thesis . . . is that what underlies our emasculation of sex is the *separation of sex from eros*. Indeed, we have set sex over *against* eros, used sex precisely to avoid the anxiety-creating involvements of eros. . . . We are in a flight from eros—and we use sex as the vehicle for the flight. Sex is the handiest drug to blot out our awareness of the anxiety creating aspects of eros. To accomplish this, we have had to define sex even more narrowly: the more we became preoccupied with sex, the more truncated and shrunken became the human experience to which it referred. We fly to *the sensation of sex in order to avoid the passion of eros.*[13]

Our culture has lost the true life-giving sense of eros. In fact, eros has become a dirty word, indicating lust, deviancy, and carnal degradation. This is, to say the least, unfortunate. Pointing out how our society has separated sex from love, Rollo May distinguishes sex and eros:

> Sex can be defined fairly adequately in physiological terms as consisting of the building up of bodily tensions and their release. Eros, in contrast, is the experiencing of the personal intentions and meaning of the act. Whereas sex is a rhythm of stimulus and response, eros is a state of being . . . eros seeks union with the other person in delight and passion, and the procreating of new dimensions of experience which broaden and deepen the being of both persons." [14]

Obviously, eros is what is missing in our neopuritanism, in our attention to sex manuals, and in our sexual technology that places such great weight on technique in sexual relations. The erotic element is repressed—the passion, the desire for union in aesthetic as well as physiological terms, the desire for creativity, expression, commitment, and spontaneity. Sex without the feelings, values, and emotions of eros may be caricatured by two machines in bed programming orgasm to fully satisfy. As May says, it is not physical nakedness which gives us pause, but spiritual-mental-emotional nakedness. The "machines" may indeed be naked; yet there is a "chastity belt" drawn tight around the "inner self" of the person who avoids the passion of eros. The "chastity belt" hides the heart, not the genitalia.

Eros is a release of libido and affect, sharing and communication. Eros is the deep inner urge to "know" the other, much as the ancient Hebrew word for "know" means sexual knowledge. Yet to "know" only sexually is not to know fully. Eros is the physical abandon of lovers who are enabled to abandon because they care, feel, and trust.

Case Study 7

Paul is 20 years old, unmarried, and considers himself to be liberated from the binds of conventional middle-class morality.

"I made this appointment because I'm having trouble with a problem," remarked Paul to the counselor. "I've had all kinds of girls . . . whores, pick-ups, townees, and some real nice bitches here on the campus. As far as I'm concerned the townees put out the best. They really know how to make a guy go out of his mind. Well, everything seemed to be going along fine until the other day. For some time now I've been dating this girl who I really like—kinda—and, well, she's a little bit different. I've had sex with her but when I did I had trouble getting an erection—Imagine that! Say, you aren't going to write this down or report me, are you? Like I was saying, this girl did something to me I can't seem to get out of my mind. I even started to feel jealous when she told me she had had sex with some other guy. The thing that really gets me though is that now I'm having trouble making it with townees. I don't seem to get very excited . . . and after it's over I get this empty feeling like all it amounted to was a lot of nothing."

On a subsequent visit to the counselor, Paul stated: "I never would have believed it but I think I've discovered there is more to sex than just orgasm. Late last week I couldn't make it with a townee. Hell! I just couldn't pull it off. Was I ever disgusted with myself. What would people think? The guys! Wow! So of course I told a pack of lies to the guys but inside I was miserable. Then the weekend—and that chick I told you about, the one who I got jealous about when I found out she had sex with another guy, well, we had the most fantastic weekend. We did everything—we ate together, went swimming, to the movies, studied together, went horseback riding, we really . . . (pause) we really opened up to each other . . . like it was great . . . I really emptied my guts to her and she to me. I never felt so close to another human being in my whole life. We had sex a couple times and it was the greatest I ever had. For the first time in my life I felt I really *loved* a girl. We were so close."

Why is Paul so intent on sexual experiences? What does the variety of sex partners imply about his view of sex? What kind of self-concept does Paul have? What does sexual conquest do for Paul's sense of self and his feelings of masculinity? What is the payoff for Paul in revealing his sexual prowess to his male friends? What relationship might there be between Paul's feelings and his occasional impotency?

The case study serves our purposes in pointing out that Paul had been experiencing many facets of libidinous love. His thoughts about his weekend experience gives testimony to the development of an erotic type of love. We can begin to sense the blending of libido, eros, philos, and agape. Paul experienced a psychic intimacy with a female which not only had a carry-over into the passion-filled eros but included elements of philos and agape. Paul experienced a "spiritual nakedness" for the first time in his life.

Marriage as a Configuration

We noted in Chapter 3 that sex was a pleasure in and of itself and that this intrinsic pleasure is its own meaning with its own value. We further noted that there can be added value and meaning if a number of values are congruent with each other and form a configuration that imparts a meaning to a whole that is greater than the sum of its parts. Consequently there are, let us say, several values a person holds, each intrinsically meaningful. As long as values do not conflict with each other—are congruent—they may complement each other so as to form a configuration in which the whole is greater than the intrinsic meaning of any of the individual parts.

Seen in this light, we can say that there is a separate, identifiable, intrinsic value in the libidinous sexual expression, and the erotic, philial, and agape forms of love. Further, when these four kinds of love are congruent they form a configuration which bestows a "higher" meaning to the total relationship. In short, we are saying that the coming together of sex, romance, and marriage can be accomplished if, instead of relying on either a straight sexual concept of love or a straight romantic concept of love, the two partners place sex, eros, philos, and agape into a congruent relationship which then forms a configuration—an intimate, growing relationship. If the four kinds of love are not congruent—for example, if eros is lacking with one's spouse and he relieves his sexual drive with third parties, with or without eros—then the several kinds of love are not being satisfied in a single marital configuration. Furthermore, if eros or the libido-type love is lacking with one's mate and if this lack is *not* fulfilled in extramarital relations, there is still *no marital configuration* of libido, eros, philos, and agape.

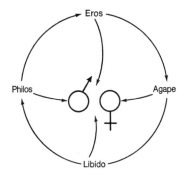

Figure 4–1
A Configuration in which
the Four Kinds of Love Are Congruent

There is little question that value "trade-offs" need to be arranged if a configuration including extramarital sex is considered to be desirable. Or one may deliberately trade off opportunities to have extramarital sexual relations (of the sexual or erotic types) in order to preserve the value of a configuration. Countless men and women make this trade-off, and countless others do not. Still others have, at one time in their life, failed to make a trade-off and opted instead for the intrinsic meaning resulting from an experience with an extramarital partner only to discover that there was a weakening of the extrinsic meaning which the marital relationship had provided.

Seen in this light the entire area of sexual ethics may be seen as a question of the value relationships and value hierarchy set up by each couple. The entire idea of commitment, trust, sex, and marriage will be a totally unacceptable option for many people because they do not hold the particular configuration to be something of value. Others will opt for utilitarian marriages in order that a partial congruency may exist, even if not a fully satisfying configuration.

Albert Ellis, writing on the pros and cons of adultery, suggests that the person who has established a marital relationship of value and meaning may well tread lightly concerning adultery since to commit adultery basically implies an adulteration, or a diluting of something containing value.[15] By our analysis, it is the configuration in which adultery takes place that is important. The central concern is whether the relationship has been diluted, thus preventing the values from being wholly congruent and precluding an extrinsic meaning for the configuration.

An Afterword

There will be many who protest the burial of romance. So be it. We do want to emphasize that while the romantic emphasis is best left in the state of *rigor mortis,* the marital configuration need not preclude moonlight, candlelight, roses, wine, and other "romantic trappings." We have consistently suggested that eros involves tenderness and commitment, affection and mystique as well as sexual desire. Indeed, the couple that seeks to actualize the marital relationship will use variety, spontaneity, and imagination to this end. We are suggesting, however, that these qualities imply the death of a movement known as *romanticism,* which at heart is a philosophy of relationships between the sexes based on false hopes, unrealistic and idealistic expectations; consequently, it is a breeding ground for disillusionment, disenchantment, disappointment, resentment, and despair.

---

5   Conflict Resolution: An Entrée into the Self

How does our culture feel about interpersonal conflict? Is the existence or nonexistence of conflict a moral consideration? In what forms do suppressed and repressed conflict appear? What can avoidance of conflict do to a marital relationship? Is there any benefit to be gained from openly confronting conflict? How can transactional analysis be applied to marital conflict? What forms of communication are conducive to growth-producing communication between spouses?

There is a popular societal taboo against conflict, particularly marital conflict. The taboo is not explicit; it is implicit. The word *conflict* conjures up negative connotations due to our historical view that conflict is morally wrong.

Conflict as a Fact of Life

Marital interaction, parental interaction with children and teenagers, sibling interaction, three-generational familial interaction, as well as all other interpersonal relationships are potentially conflict-laden. A cultural tradition which, for whatever historically conditioned reasons, considers conflict morally wrong will encourage the suppression and repression of conflict, thus laying a foundation for misunderstanding, resentment, anger, hostility, bitterness, hatred, and misplaced aggression.

Although many cultures as well as our own endow conflict with moral or immoral connotations, we shall take the position that conflict itself is amoral—that is, without moral value. In other words, we see conflict as a neutral phenomenon; it is how one looks upon conflict and how one handles it that gives it a positive or negative value. If, for example, a married couple is socialized to believe that argument is wrong, that the voicing of disagreement is to be avoided, and that the essence of marriage is to create and maintain harmony at any price, then not only will this couple probably claim that neither of them ever remembers an unkind word between their parents, but they will feel guilt that their own marital relationship is not beautiful or perfect. They will probably feel conflict and sense their underlying hostility, but they will not be able to do anything about it except be miserable, for, after all, conflict implies fighting and fighting is wrong! Isn't it?

Perhaps the most unfortunate result of this kind of socialization is the fact that the children of this couple will now in turn be deprived of any viable models of how to face and deal with conflict in a creative, growth-producing, love-filling way.

The root of this negative attitude toward conflict is the popular assumption that love is the polar opposite of hate. At times it may be. At other times, the line between love and hate is a very fine line, and until the negative feelings are allowed expression there is a diminution of the positive feelings as well. This state of affairs leads many couples to conclude: "We feel nothing toward each other, neither love nor hate." Naturally, for when the negative is repressed so will be the positive. "Our love has died," is an expression often heard by marriage counselors and psychotherapists. Why not, for the experience of "dying love" is in part the experience of the denial of feelings, first the negative, and then as a consequence, the positive. Rollo May has described this dynamic:

> A curious thing which never fails to surprise persons in therapy is that after admitting their anger, animosity, and even hatred for a spouse and berating him or her during the hour, they end up with feelings of love toward this partner. A patient may have come in smoldering with negative feelings but resolved, partly unconsciously, to keep these, as a good gentleman does, to himself; but he finds that he represses the love for the partner at the same time as he suppresses his aggression . . . the positive cannot come out until the negative does also. . . . Hate and love are not polar opposites; they go together, particularly in transitional ages like ours.[1]

The following case study illustrates more concretely the effects of forbidding oneself negative feelings.

Case Study 8

Kathy and John have been married for four years. They have come to the counselor only after Kathy has insisted that they do so.

John: I am afraid I don't love Kathy. I don't know how or why but the feelings I used to have are gone. I try to recreate them but . . . well, it just doesn't work. Sometimes I force myself to be loving but then it seems . . . like . . . pow! . . . she turns around and does something to really turn me off! One of these days I'm afraid I'm really going to unload on Kathy.

Kathy: Unload what?

John: Well, just . . . Oh forget it!

Kathy: No! *Unload what?* I suppose you think I'm just feeling good about you all the time. Well, I'm not! You've got me so mixed up and confused I don't know how I feel or what I think. Lately, you just make me sick—acting like a hurt little boy if you don't get everything your way, clamming up, pouting and sulking.

John: You sure put your finger on it. How else am I supposed to feel when you put me down? You're the one who seems to have to get her own way. You act like no one can handle the money as well as you . . . You insist on doing things with *your* friends. You act like sex is a bore and you parcel it out like it was rationed. You undermine everything I try to do with the kids. The fact is, I think sometimes your judgment in handling them stinks . . .

 Kathy: I suppose you're an expert!

 John: I think you're too easy on them.

And here we go with gunnysacking—the unloading of past grievances. At best, gunnysacking provides a release of pent-up feelings, an unleashing of the negative feelings which have been put down into the gunnysack for safekeeping, but which end up being used as ammunition at some later time. At worst, gunnysacking provides a decoy to get negative feelings out in the open, even if they are not the real cause of the present impasse. If Kathy and John are encouraged to unload on each other on deeper levels, they may succeed in getting at some of their real resentments. And these negative feelings have been dammed up so long that the positive "love" feelings have correspondingly diminished. No therapist would be surprised if at one of the next counseling sessions John would say: "I'm beginning to feel love for Kathy again. I don't seem to have as much resentment . . . and I'm not even trying to make myself be loving."

George R. Bach, who has written *The Intimate Enemy* (subtitled "How to fight fair in love and marriage") has called attention to dirty fighters, sick fighters, fighting for intimacy, and training lovers to be fighters. Bach says:

> Contrary to folklore, the existence of hostility and conflict is not necessarily a sign that love is waning. As often as not, an upsurge of hate may signal a deepening of true intimacy; it is when neither love nor hate can move a partner that a relationship is deteriorating. Typically, one partner then gives up the other as a "lost cause" or shrugs him off ("I couldn't care less"). Indifference to a partner's anger and hate is a surer sign of a deteriorating relationship than is indifference to love.[2]

Thus, it is more correct to say that indifference is the polar opposite of both love and hate. Outright rejection is often easier to accept than being ignored or treated indifferently as though one were not there!

Seen in this light, it is clear that the creative facing of conflict is an absolute necessity in marital relations. In fact, considering that previous generations embraced the ethical and moral concept of "honesty," we may wonder how honest our ancestors were as they avoided conflict like the plague. This is dishonest! Perhaps their dishonesty may be excused in that they were thoroughly conditioned in the belief that conflict was an evil thing. Nevertheless, the avoidance of conflict is, at heart, a dishonest stance in interpersonal relationships.

For lessons in "how to fight fair in love and marriage," as Bach puts it, the reader is referred to his book. Our concern here is to examine the nature of intrapsychic and interpsychic conflict and then to outline a system of **transactional analysis** which will, hopefully, enable the reader to understand the nature of his own intrapersonal and interpersonal communications. Our premise is that only as a person understands the nature of his inner conflicts is he able to deal creatively with his interpersonal conflicts. To this end, transactional analysis will be used as an entrée into the self.

Intrapsychic and Interpsychic Conflict

Intrapsychic conflict is that conflict within the self which arises from our drives, instincts, and values pulling against each other. Classical psychoanalysis (Freud) posits the fundamental conflict as one between the id and the superego. Psychoanalytical and **neopsychoanalytical theory** since Freud has stressed the centrality of intrapsychic conflict as the essential dynamic of neurotic behavior. Intrapsychic conflict is one of the precursors of interpsychic conflict. These two terms do not refer to phenomena existing within the self but are symbolic references to libidinous (instinctual) energy and the internalized voice of parents and society (conscience). Ideally, the ego is sufficiently strong enough to be the arbiter between the id (seeking pleasure) and the superego (demanding perfection). The ego takes account of the reality of the core self of the person; the degree of strength and maturity of the ego determines the degree of control the superego is allowed to exercise over the instinctual libidinous drives. Frankl has

---

Transactional analysis. A type of psychotherapy based on the study and analysis of the communication, metacommunication, and symbolic communication (transactions) between two people.

Neopsychoanalytical theory. Expansion and reinterpretation of Freud's discoveries based on new empirical and clinical evidence. Especially refers to the theories of Karen Horney, Harry Stack Sullivan and Erich Fromm.

pointed out that there is another kind of conflict besides this conflict of drives and instincts (which result in what he terms "psychogenic neurosis"). He suggests that anxiety ("noogenic neurosis") also arises from "conflicts between various values; in other words, from moral conflicts or, to speak in a more general way, from spiritual problems." [3]

An internal conflict can focus on anything that encounters resistance when attempts are made to incorporate it or make it acceptable to the self. Since facing conflict creates unpleasant feelings of tension and anxiety, individuals develop conscious or unconscious methods of handling conflict. One method is to suppress it—that is, to consciously put it in the back of one's mind and deliberately decide not to deal with it. Repression, on the other hand, is an unconscious process of blocking out the conflict so that it doesn't come out into the open, into consciousness. However, material repressed in the unconscious still exerts a powerful influence on us, for repression can cause conflict to be disguised in the form of compulsions, obsessions, anxiety, and depression.

If a person is torn within, consciously or unconsciously, he will be unable to deal with conflicts on the interpersonal (interpsychic) level. People who have dealt successfully with their inner conflicts are able to address themselves to interpersonal conflict in a reasonably creative, autonomous, and spontaneous manner. Let us caution, however, that to experience internal conflict is to be human. There can be no counsel of perfection about our inner conflicts; our humanity is such that we are capable of emotionality *and* rationality. We experience drives, desires, feelings, and pleasures; we also experience meaning and meaninglessness, value and worthlessness, intelligence and stupidity. Our intellect can serve us in conflict avoidance as well as in conflict resolution. For example, through *rationalization* one can refer to plausible reasons for his behavior to avoid facing the real reasons; or a person can unconsciously *project* his own traits on another person so that he won't have to see them in himself; or through *transference* an individual might transfer his feelings toward a significant person in his life (particularly parents) to another person. All of these are conflict-avoidance games we play with ourselves.

Case Study 9

George and Betty have been going together for almost a year. Their relationship has been a deep and rewarding experience for both of them. Lately, however, George has become picky, hypercriti-

cal, and sensitive to things Betty says and does. George has decided
to talk to a counselor about his relationship with Betty.

"I don't know what it is, but everything she does bugs me. I get
angry when she tries to plan an evening or a weekend. Then when
she doesn't offer her opinions about what we're going to do I feel she
doesn't care. We're saving money for our marriage and then she
comes up with expensive ideas on how to spend it. Lately, no matter
what it is, I react negatively. The other day for instance . . . we were
going for a walk downtown and she started window shopping—you
know, saying how much she'd like this dress or that coat. I found
myself getting critical and hostile. I felt like . . . well, like here was a
person who was going to try to manipulate me. (Pause) A couple of
weeks ago I wanted her to make over me a little. I had seen some girl
really pouring a lot of love onto a guy and it struck me that Betty
never makes over me that way. So when I saw her I noted her reactions. She sure was a loser compared to that girl I had seen. And we
argue a lot—no matter what we are discussing I end up disagreeing
with her. You know—like if she says it's a groovy flick I'll take the
opposite approach. If she thinks Vietnam is stupid, I find myself defending our commitment. . . . Yet I love her. I still want to marry
her! Why do I keep reacting to her the way I do?"

There is, of course, no simple answer to George's question, "Why
do I keep reacting to her the way I do?" Every couple needs to work
through their interpersonal reactions, and no relationship is entirely
free of personality quirks or idiosyncrasies. Basically, however, it may
be that George's basic conflict is intrapsychic, or inside himself. He
reveals some contradictory tendencies. On the one hand, he fears
being manipulated, but he is not altogether sure what constitutes manipulation by Betty. He wants to be made over; yet the result is that
he creates a "test" for Betty as if he says to himself, "I'll watch her
every move and see how unsatisfyingly she responds." Of course,
under these conditions, Betty can't do anything but lose. She doesn't
know the name of the game George is playing. George finds himself
opposing Betty no matter what the issue. I would suggest that the
main conflict is in George himself, not in his relationship with Betty.
George has some deeply hidden anxiety and hostility. He is not nearly
as autonomous and self-directing as he probably pictures himself. One
possible explanation is that George is using transference; he is interacting with and responding to Betty as if he were still fighting his

mother. George appears to be easily threatened by Betty and yet, at the same time, he looks to her for reassurance and overt displays of affection. (Why can't you be like her?) Thus, George's problem is intrapsychic, a function of his personal development and environmental conditioning. How and to what extent George sees through and handles his intrapsychic problems will determine the kind and quality of relationship he has with Betty or any other prospective mate.

Interpsychic or interpersonal conflict is the more obvious kind of conflict in that it occurs between two people. It is this kind of conflict that has been regarded as taboo within marriage. According to this view, a husband and wife should not have conflict, even though familial conflict between parents and children is considered normal and acceptable. Even this conflict is not very comfortable for society; witness the labeling of intergenerational conflict as the "generation gap." Could it be that the term "gap" is a way to avoid calling it "conflict"? And if it is a conflict, is it a conflict of drives and instincts, or is it a conflict of values, meanings, and purpose? One may suspect that a great deal of what is called "campus unrest" today is none other than youth in conflict with a value system which they no longer sense as viable.

Interpersonal conflict may focus on trivial, inconsequential things or it may focus on major issues. Within marriage, the little inconsequential things may serve as decoys for the actual source of conflict. Much of the pent-up hostility of marital partners is expressed in passive ways or is displaced to inappropriate objects. Hence the designation, "passive-aggressive personality" is given to those who aggress passively, perhaps by being unduly critical, by faultfinding, or by "nitpicking." When aggressive, hostile feelings are displaced, we recognize it as a form of "scapegoating." There is a well-defined pecking order in our society which designates in no uncertain terms who may be the legitimate object of our displaced hostility feelings. The unfortunate fact is that neither displacement nor passive-aggressiveness need be operative if we could take seriously the reality of conflict and learn how to deal with it maturely and creatively.

Let us turn from our discussion of intrapsychic and interpsychic conflict to a consideration of a method of self-study which may serve as a "handle" for creatively working through conflict. The underlying assumption is, of course, that conflict is a human reality, and as such amoral, and that as we become proficient in understanding and handling the intrapsychic conflicts, we will be free to become equally proficient at understanding and working through our interpsychic conflicts.

Transactional Analysis

If marriage is to be thought of as a "human-actualizing contract" [4] then it is important that both parties commit themselves, implicitly or explicitly, to the growth model of marital interaction and enrichment. Such a commitment implies a willingness to face conflict in a creative way. Transactional analysis is one method which may help us to do just that. It is a method for achieving self-understanding in order to further the process of growth toward self-actualization.

Eric Berne's *Games People Play* became a bestseller, but unfortunately, its popularity seemed to be based on public fascination with the games rather than on the dynamics underlying the games. [5] Dr. Thomas Harris worked closely with Dr. Berne as one of the original members of the San Francisco Social Psychiatry Seminars. Harris' contribution to transactional analysis is entitled *I'm OK—You're OK*.

Unlike psychoanalysis, which builds on concepts of energies in the self (superego, ego, and id), Harris names what he considers real parts of the personality—the Parent, the Child, and the Adult.

> Continual observation has supported the assumption that these three states exist in all people. It is as if in each person there is the same little person he was when he was three years old. There are also within him his own parents. These states are audio-visual recordings in the brain of actual experiences of internal and external events, the most significant of which happened during the first five years of life. There is a third state, different from these two. The first two are called Parent and Child, and the third, Adult. [6]

The Parent is like a video tape recorder which recorded all the information available to it throughout childhood without editing, scrutinizing, or judging. Thus, the Parent is the "taught" way of life with which we were carefully indoctrinated during those early years, especially during the first five years of life.

> The Parent is a huge collection of recordings in the brain of unquestioned or imposed external data perceived by a person in his

early years, a period which we have designated roughly as the first five years of life. . . . The name Parent is the most descriptive of this data inasmuch as the most significant "tapes" are those provided by the example and pronouncements of his own real parents or parent substitutes. Everything the child saw his parents do and everything he heard them say is recorded in the Parent.[7]

The Parent is the source of rules, laws, standards, proscriptions, prescriptions, frowns, smiles, praise, approval and disapproval. According to Harris, "The significant point is that whether these rules are good or bad in the light of a reasonable ethic, they are recorded as *truth* from the source of all security, the people who are 'six feet tall' at a time when it is important to the two-foot-tall child that he please and obey them. It is a permanent recording. A person cannot erase it. It is available for replay throughout life." [8]

The Child is also a recording, which is made simultaneously with the Parent recording. However, it is a recording of feelings—what the child feels as he sees and hears, as he experiences, and as he understands or doesn't understand. The child is two feet tall as he absorbs and responds to his six-feet-tall parents. "Since the little person has no vocabulary during the most critical of his early experiences, most of his reactions are *feelings*. We must keep in mind his situation in these early years. He is small, he is dependent, he is inept, he is clumsy, he has no words with which to construct meanings." [9] If the Parent is the "taught" way of life, the Child may be labeled the "felt" way of life. There are many positive feelings that the child felt, which became the basis of his feelings of joy, pleasure, happiness, and spontaneity. The negative feelings, however, are the ones that seem to cause the difficulty.

> The predominant by-product of the frustrating, civilizing process is negative feelings. On the basis of these feelings the little person early concludes, "I'm NOT OK." We call this comprehensive self-estimate the NOT OK, or the NOT OK Child. This conclusion and the continual experiencing of the unhappy feelings which led to it and confirm it are recorded permanently in the brain and cannot be erased. This permanent recording is the residue of having been a child. Any child. Even the child of kind, loving, well-meaning parents. It is the *situation of childhood* and *not* the intention of the parents which produces the problem. . . . As in the case of the Parent,

the Child is a state into which a person may be transferred at almost any time in his current transactions. There are many things that can happen to us today which recreate the situation of childhood and bring on the same feelings we felt then.[10]

The third intrapsychic phenomenon is called the Adult. The Adult is essentially our "thought" way of life, in that the Adult is like a computer which gathers and processes data fed through it by the Parent and the Child.

The ten-month-old has found he is able to do something which grows from his own awareness and original thought. This self-actual-ization is the beginning of the Adult. . . . Adult data accumulates as a result of the child's ability to find out for himself what is different about life from the "taught concept" of life in his Parent and the "felt concept" of life in his Child. The Adult develops a "thought concept" of life based on data gathering and data processing.[11]

The Adult does reality testing and probability estimating. He checks out the Parent data to see if they are valid or invalid, applicable today or out-dated, and in this light he determines how to accept and handle the feelings of the Child. As Harris says, ". . . the understanding of how the original situation of childhood produced so many NOT OK recordings of this type can free us of their continual replay in the present. *We cannot erase the recording, but we can choose to turn it off!*" [12]

Using these three intrapsychic phenomena we can visualize such conflict-producing situations as the contamination of the Adult by the Parent (leading to prejudice), the contamination of the Adult by the Child (leading to delusion), a Parent-contaminated Adult with a blocked-out Child, a Child-contaminated Adult with a blocked-out Parent, and a blocked-out or decommissioned Adult, which is a psychotic state completely out of touch with reality.

Harris describes four basic life positions. First there is "I'm Not OK—You're OK," which "is the universal position of early childhood, being the infant's logical conclusion from the situation of birth and infancy." [13] Harris concludes that all children experience this position, with no exceptions. The self-image depends, even at this age, on the self-estimate as reflected by others toward the infant. The infant looks up to the big, tall parents and is reminded of his own smallness, weakness, and helplessness. Such writers as Alfred Adler, Harry Stack Sullivan, Erich Fromm, and Karen Horney describe this same other-oriented state of infancy, although in different terms.

Only *some* children adopt the second position, which usually occurs during the second year of life. The second position which is really a "gravitation toward," says, "I'm Not OK—You're Not OK." While the first position brought **stroking** to the infant, the second position does not. "Life, which in the first year had some comforts, now has none. The stroking has disappeared. If this state of abandonment and difficulty continues without relief through the second year of life, the child concludes "I'm Not OK—You're Not OK." In this position the Adult stops developing since one of its primary functions—getting strokes—is thwarted in that there is no source of stroking. A person in this position gives up. There is no hope." [14] In essence, the child who gravitates to this position is saying, "I'm no good, but you're no good either." His experiences make him feel worthless, and there is no "significant other" who can be trusted and counted on.

The third position is a much different alternative from the second.

> A child who is brutalized long enough by the parents he initially felt were OK will switch positions to the third, or criminal position: I'm OK—You're Not OK. . . . The tragedy, for himself and for society, is that he goes through life refusing to look inward. He is unable to be objective about his own complicity in what happens to him. It is always "their fault." It's "all them." Incorrigible criminals occupy this position. They are the persons "without a conscience" who are convinced that they are OK no matter what they do and that the total fault in every situation lies in others.[15]

The fourth position is the goal of transactional analysis.

> There is a fourth position, wherein lies our hope. It is the I'm OK —You're OK position. There is a qualitative difference between the

---

Stroking. A term used in transactional analysis to refer to the psychological rewards resulting from physical, verbal, and symbolic praising from others. Basically, it consists of significant others telling the self "You are OK. You are worthwhile. You are lovable."

first three positions and the fourth position. The first three are un-conscious, having been made early in life. I'm Not OK—You're OK came first and persists for most people throughout life. For certain extremely unfortunate children this position was changed to positions two and three. By the third year of life one of these positions is fixed in every person. . . . The fourth position, I'm OK—You're OK, because it is a conscious and verbal decision, can include not only an infinitely greater amount of information about the individ-ual and others, but also the incorporation of not-yet-experienced possibilities which exist in the abstractions of philosophy and reli-gion. *The first three positions are based on feelings. The fourth is based on thought, faith, and the wager of action. . . . We do not drift into a new position. It is a decision we make.*[16]

Positions two and three are assumed by a very small percentage of the population. A high percentage of people remain in position one all their life, "I'm not OK—You're OK." Most people deal with their Not OK feelings by playing games. Each game has some sort of emo-tional pay-off, usually hidden or implicit. The more common games include: "Mine is better than yours"; "If it weren't for you . . ."; "Ain't it awful"; "Look what you did to me"; "Look what you made me do"; and "Look how hard I tried."

Transactional analysis is a tool, a method of looking at the verbal and nonverbal transactions between people in order to determine where the transaction originated. Some originate in the Not OK Child. Some originate in the Parent. Hopefully, most transactions originate in the Adult. If a person had unpleasant feelings as a child of being rejected or criticized, it is not at all unlikely that in his grown years he still cannot handle rejection or criticism. The old feelings—or recordings—play their old familiar tune: We would say his Not OK Child is "hooked." When our children ask us, after we have given an authoritative pronouncement on the acceptable limits to length of hair, "Who put that into your head?" we may discover after careful examination and self-scrutiny that we are dispensing archaic Parent data which has not been analyzed by our Adult computer. By the same token, we may feed into the computer "I don't like long hair! I was raised differently! I guess I'm a little old-fashioned! Nevertheless, the standard will be this: If you want to wear long hair then I expect it to be combed and clean." In this case, although the child may not feel he has won anything, the transaction is a result of his father's using his own Adult computer, rather than blind repetition of archaic (and maybe faulty) Parent data.

Transactional analysis is a method of introspection that can serve as a framework for a great variety of psychological and therapeutic theories. Furthermore, the method advocated by Harris makes it possible to discover one's own games and to consciously adopt the fourth position. *This is not easy to do.* Nevertheless, when we realize that the Not OK feelings will never be erased, but that as adults we can refuse to listen to them, then the game-playing strategy can be discarded. Harris says about this:

> The only way people get well or become OK is to expose the childhood predicament underlying the first three positions. . . . it is essential to understand that I'm OK—You're OK is a *position and not a feeling.* The Not OK recordings in the Child are not erased by a decision in the present. The task at hand is how to start a collection of recordings which play OK outcomes to transactions, successes in terms of correct probability estimating, successes in terms of integrated actions which make sense, which are programmed by the Adult, and not by the Parent or Child, successes based on an ethic which can be supported rationally.[17]

Slowly, our Adult will discover that we need not go through life trying to bandage up our wounded "Not OK" Child. Instead, we can use what Parent and Child data we decide is meaningful, relevant, and appropriate after we have put it through our own Adult computer.

Conflict Resolution: Adult-Adult

The tension between the Not OK Child and the Parent is usually, in one way or another, the root cause of intrapsychic and interpsychic conflict. Not OK feelings take the form of insecurity, inferiority, helplessness, worthlessness, shame, doubt, and guilt. Not OK-ness is, as Harris has pointed out, the inevitable result of early childhood and the dependency it implies. The intrapsychic conflict which the Not OK person experiences is a continuation of the struggle to achieve self-trust and autonomy. In this connection, Horney has pointed out that when a person fails to learn self-trust and consequently lacks autonomy he will likely move toward others, trying to win their praise, approval, and affection, taking great care to conceal any resentment or hostility.[18] He is afraid of rejection or rebuff, and hence is overly sensitive to the remarks and opinions of others. The Not OK Adult (translated to Horney's terms) may move "against others" instead of "toward" them, putting himself one-up and adopting a manipulative, controlling stance so that he can exercise power over others. A third tact may be to move "away" from others by seeking solitude as a haven of security from the risks of intimacy. Horney notes that everyone uses these three patterns and that the healthy person keeps all three in balance while the neurotic usually leans heavily on one of the three to the exclusion of the other two.

Transactional analysis can help the Adult to see and feel his Not OK child at work. Once we learn to see clearly the Parent and Child working within us we can consciously decide to disallow the P and C recordings. This, however, is an Adult decision. When the Adult is in control of the situation the transaction may include updating P and C data. The Adult does not need to play games which in one way or another (one-downsmanship, one-upmanship, escapism) are calculated to control and manipulate others. In his book *Man, the Manipulator*, Everett Shostrom talks about "Top-Dog" and "Under-Dog," making the same point that we assume these positions in order to manipulate and control others.[19]

The challenge in transactional analysis is to pinpoint the origin of a thought, a feeling, or a communication. If the point of origin is in our Parent or Child then we can see it, identify it or label it, and proceed to consciously move into our Adult by updating the Parent or Child data in order to determine if it is relevant today. If it is not, then the Adult acknowledges it to himself: if it is relevant, then the material still needs to be analyzed by the Adult computer and placed into proper perspective. The situation may call for the Adult to face the conflict using clear communication directed to the Adult of the other person, whether the other person is a parent, a spouse, or a friend. If this is the case the chances are increased that a resolution of the conflict may be forthcoming. Conflict resolution is possible only when the Adults of both people are communicating. If I direct my communication to the Child of another person, and if that Child responds to my Adult, we do have a complementary transaction, but conflict resolution will be difficult because the Child is not able to handle conflict as the Adult can. It is the Child that is so easily threatened.

If the transaction is not complementary—that is, if the Parent addresses the Child and the Child responds to the Child, there is a

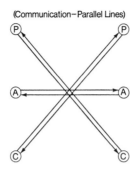

(Communication–Parallel Lines)

Figure 5–1
Complementary Transactions

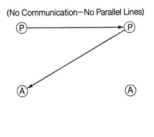

(No Communication–No Parallel Lines)

Figure 5–2
A Noncomplementary Transaction

breakdown of communication. Figure 5–1 illustrates complementary transactions among Parent (P), Child (C), and Adult (A) of two people. Complementary transactions always have parallel lines (communication); noncomplementary transactions do not, as illustrated in Figure 5–2. Effective conflict resolution, however, requires not only parallel lines but parallel lines between Adult and Adult (see Figure 5–3).

In marital conflict the Parent or Child often takes over and

> . . . the whole marriage is shattered when imperfections begin to appear. Marriage is the most complicated of all human relationships. Few alliances can produce such extremes of emotion or can so

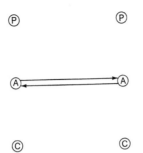

Figure 5–3
Complementary
Communication—Conflict Resolution

quickly travel from professions of the utmost bliss to that cold, terminal legal write-off, mental cruelty. When one stops to consider the massive content of archaic data which each partner brings to the marriage through the continuing contribution of his Parent and Child, one can readily see the necessity of an emancipated Adult in each to make this relationship work.[20]

Marital Actualization and the OK Child

Transactional analysis could be a most effective tool in helping to bring about self-actualizing marriage, since the Not OK Child is the source of most illegitimate needs that individuals bring to a relationship (see Chapter 2). The roots of marital disillusionment can be traced, in part, to the lack of using the Adult computer when confronted with legal, moral, traditional, and societal expectations of marriage. The socialization of the young is a Parent function, and much of that teaching applies to masculinity/femininity expectations and husband/wife roles. The data absorbed by the Child may be valid or invalid, moralistic or rooted in carefully considered values. The reaction of spouse to spouse often never gets beyond the Child-Child stage of communication, as each spouse tries to get stroking from the other or to play a game of one-upmanship. The desire for romantic love may well be the "crying" of the Not OK Child seeking for new assurance and promises of affection, all because the Not OK Child has consistently allowed other people to do the "valuating," the placing and ascribing of value and worth upon the individual.

Self-fulfillment and the process of actualizing oneself would seem to be a remote possibility if one had no way to get in touch with the source of his feelings, reactions, attitudes, and behavior. The Not OK Child is wallowing in "D" (deficiency) needs; "Being" needs can be met only by those who make a conscious decision to embrace the I'm OK—You're OK position (see Chapter 2). The "neurotic" need for affection, about which Horney writes, is the Not OK Child asking for stroking by playing various games and employing various strategies and maneuvers. The Not OK Child may also employ sex as a means of obtaining stroking; however, such acting out of feelings of anger, hostility, resentment, and aggression in the sexual sphere is, as we have seen, a very questionable type of human sexuality.

When the spouses can interact with each other on the "I'm OK—You're OK" basis they are free to work with Adult data rather than archaic Parent-Child data. They are free to deal with present reality unhampered by past "Not OK" feelings. Instead of communication running between the Parent of one spouse to the Child of the other spouse or vice versa, growth-producing communication should be between Adult and Adult. Indeed, Adult-Adult communication is an absolute prerequisite for a self-actualizing marital relationship, at least as a *basic life stance*. Obviously, no one can speak as an Adult all the time; there will be times of backsliding and momentary returns to the Parent and Child positions.

Only when human beings are free to be themselves, free from the tyrannical Parent which beats upon and threatens the Child, can they have an actualizing marriage. Freedom *from* is a prerequisite for freedom *to*. We cannot "be what we are" until we are somewhat at peace (reconciled) with what we were. Actualizing selves are not paragons of perfection; they are human beings who seek to express and fulfill their humanity.

Two self-actualizing people will not automatically have a self-actualizing marriage, but the prerequisites are partially met. Marriage, even with self-actualizing partners, begs for a certain amount of role definition and clarification. Male and female role models from the early years may return to plague the partners; this is to be expected. Idealized self-images and idealized spouse images often need to be exposed and frankly labeled. The premise still holds, however, that until an individual attains freedom from the archaic tyranny of the Parent and Child, he is not free to be himself.

Conflict Defused but Unresolved

Conflict resolution requires a relationship between mates who are basically in the "I'm OK—You're OK" position and communicating with the Adult components of their personalities. Yet, even a complementary transaction between Adults is no guarantee that a given conflict will be resolved. There are times when the partners can simply proceed no further. If the unresolved conflict is being handled by Adults, and if the source of conflict is sufficiently important to each person that living together is no longer feasible, then sometimes divorce is the only alternative, even with Adult-Adult people.

If the conflict is not resolvable and if it is defined as not being of absolutely crucial importance, then two Adult-Adult people may simply have to accept the fact that they cannot resolve that particular issue. In this case, the conflict is at least defused. Stalemate need not be harmful providing the conflict has been adequately dealt with. The danger of unfaced conflict lies primarily in the process of conflict denial, suppression, or repression. In these situations, the conflict cannot be defused because it is not being treated on the Adult-Adult level. Such denied and displaced conflict tends to create anger, hostility, resentment, anxiety, depression, and aggression. Defused conflict, although not resolved, at least loses its potential to do destructive work in a hidden or underground way. It is always the repressed and the denied that comes back to drive the person; unresolved conflict, once defused, has little power to do harm if the partners are able to accept the stalemate in a mature Adult-Adult manner.

---

6   Rigor Morphis: Alternatives and Options

Can traditional marriage be said to be in a state of "rigor morphis"? What viable alternatives might there be to a traditional marital arrangement? Are standards of sexual exclusivity necessary to a marriage? What are the possible effects of sexual permissiveness? Of what value can a group marriage be? Is "serial monogamy" a fulfilling arrangement? In light of history, what forms of communal living and group marriage are likely to succeed or fail? Is there really anything new going on today? What are the pros and cons of a two-step marriage? Are trial marriages copouts or responsible arrangements?

Many people accuse the traditional monogamous marriage of having rigidified into unworkable expectations and roles. Thus, we coin the term *rigor* (a state of rigidity in living tissues or organs that prevents response to stimuli) *morphis* (from *morphic,* pertaining to form) to refer to structural rigidity within the marital relationship.

Those who find the marital relationship and its legal and ecclesiastical traditions in such a state of *rigor morphis* are seeking viable alternatives. This chapter will focus on the fact that this rigidity is a reality for many, and we shall examine what can be done about it. Our answer will consist of three parts: emerging nontraditional marital patterns, marriage in two stages, and in the next chapter, renewal from within.

Emerging Nontraditional Marital Patterns

A historical overview often indicates that what is viewed by one culture or era as new is, in reality, quite old. Thus, we can see that many "emerging" marital patterns are simply reemerging.

For example, the first option, monogamy with extramarital permissiveness (or permissive monogamy), is a cultural reality even without legal sanction. George P. Murdock has estimated that only 5 percent of the societies on the face of the earth—of which the United States is one—make no legal provision for sexual intercourse outside of marriage.[1] As noted in Chapter 1, the ancient Hebrews disapproved of adultery, yet there was concubinage and harlotry. To the Hebrews, adultery was sinful not so much because of sexual betrayal but because it involved taking something from another person. For example, Canaanite women who were the bounty of war were acceptable sexual partners for married Hebrew men. David's sin with Bathsheba was his taking of what rightfully belonged to another. Indeed, David solved that dilemma by military manipulation.[2] Further, the Hebrew patriarchs Abraham and Jacob had offspring by their wives' maids.[3]

Edward Hobbs has pointed out two traditions of marriage—marital permanence and **sexual exclusiveness.** The American way is to destroy marital permanence whenever the principle of sexual exclusivity is broken. Note the various state laws permitting divorce only on the

---

Sexual exclusiveness. The practice of confining one's sexual activity to one and only one mate, as opposed to sexual permissiveness which allows one to have sexual liaisons with other partners as one chooses.

grounds of adultery. Hobbs complains that we destroy the nest in order to maintain the code of sexual exclusivity, thus undermining the stability of the family structure as the pivotal security source for the maturation and socialization of the young. For this reason, Hobbs suggests that our values are backward—that instead we ought to preserve the marital union and permit sexual relationships outside the union. In effect, this arrangement would amount to a utilitarian marriage with sexual freedom for both partners. *"Thus, we are in the process of abandoning the permanence of marriage, while maintaining* (in law and in principle, even if less in reality than ever before) *its sexual exclusiveness.*[4] Indeed, this alternative is already very popular in the United States. Basically, it is one answer to the question, "Can marriage be a vital, loving, interpersonal relationship and still be sexually permissive?" For many, it cannot be both. Hence, rather than stand on sexual exclusiveness at the expense of marital and familial breakup, the stand is taken on familial unity at the expense of sexual permissiveness.

Hobbs' stand in favor of familial stability over sexual exclusivity seems to make sense in view of what is known today about child development and the importance of security and love needs. But it must also be asked, what effect does sexual permissiveness have on the solidarity and emotional health of the marriage? People will point to personal experience and come up with both answers: "Little harmful effect; it is growth-producing" and "Very negative effect; it is destructive to mutual trust." Any workable answer must hinge on one's recognition that there are two basic types of "permissive monogamy." The first type, which we shall call "utilitarian," describes the couple that chooses to remain together despite the fact that much of their positive emotionality has either been lost or is greatly diminished. As Cuber and Haroff point out, these people may once have had a very vital relationship but now it is devitalized.[5] Under these circumstances, each partner decides individually whether or not to engage in intimate relationships (both psychic and sexual) with others; such marital partners have given up the possibility of building mutual love but still cooperate in the working partnership of maintaining a home.

A second type of permissive monogamy has been receiving a great deal of attention in conjunction with the concept of "open marriage," as coined by Nena and George O'Neill in their book of the same name. The O'Neills point out that the important hallmark within open marriage is not so much sexual permissiveness as the commitment of the couple to maintain a mutually satisfying growth relationship. Partners in an open marriage seek vitality and dynamic understanding. Thus, the emphasis is taken away from the societally prescribed, role-oriented marriage contract and placed instead on an open contract created by those living under the contract. In order to achieve a nonpossessive, nonjealous, nonmanipulative, and nonintrusive relationship with each other, such traditional words as trust and fidelity are given new meaning. "Trust," as commonly used, can be a negative dare ("Just try to be unfaithful!") or a threat ("I'll never forgive you if you betray my trust.") There is a more "open" trust, however, that can have more positive effects. If the partners trust each other to be open and honest in their total relationship with one another, they can give each other the freedom to be a human being instead of a role performer and an expectation meeter. In such a relationship the traditional vow of fidelity is out of place because it is demanded as part of a closed, non-freedom-giving contract; infidelity would equal mistrust or broken trust. Ironically, the expectation for sexual fidelity to one's partner, based on trust as a threat, may destroy the very relationship it was intended to protect. Recognizing this, proponents of open marriage consider "intimate friendship" with opposite-sexed friends outside the marriage a permissible norm. Intimate friendship may include sexual and psychic intimacy, or it may involve only psychic intimacy. Whether or not partners in an open marriage actually become related in intimate friendships is up to each couple. The important point is that the *freedom* and the *right* to do so are *inherent* to the open marriage and are not considered to be an abrogation of trust or fidelity to one's mate.[6]

Another alternative to marital *rigor morphis* is called "progressive monogamy," "serial monogamy," or "monogamous polygamy." Here we have the very eventuality that Hobbs warns against. In principle, there is sexual exclusivity to one's *present* mate, but the marriage is severed in favor of a more promising one at any time. Naturally the family unit suffers. The children may have a father and several stepfathers, a mother and several stepmothers. In practice, however, many of these relationships do not begin until the youngest child has left home and the nest is empty.

Progressive monogamy is a fact of life today. Even more, it is a *legal* fact and a culturally approved fact, even though many disapprove of it and condemn it. The chief effect on the individual who marries and divorces several times seems to occur toward the later years of the life cycle. A backward glance may lead to feelings of remorse, dread, emptiness, loneliness, and despair as people fail to see meaning, purpose, richness, and depth in their past. Progressive monogamy may provide the basis for many ongoing "intrinsic" marriages, each relationship having its own value. Nevertheless, the extrinsic value that can come from the total configuration allowed by a sustained relationship is often lacking. The inability to sustain a meaningful one-to-one relationship over a long period of time may be totally unimportant to many people until they enter the later stages of the life cycle. The study of aging in the later stages of the life cycle (gerontology) may provide us with insight into the relationship between value-filled permanent liaisons and the self-concept in one's later years.

Case Study 10

Howard retired a little over six years ago. He was married four times. He got married for the first time at the age of 20, and the marriage lasted seven years, ending in divorce. Howard had three children in his first marriage. His second marriage was at age 29 and it lasted for two years, ending in the death of his wife in an auto accident. His third marriage, at the age of 32, produced two children and lasted for eighteen years. This marriage ended in divorce due to what his wife called "cruel and premeditated adultery." Howard's last marriage took place when he was 55 and lasted until a little after Howard retired; his wife and he more or less agreed that the relationship had run its course after twelve years. Howard is now talking to a counselor:

"I'm having trouble understanding myself—or life—or something . . . I go from feelings of joy and happiness to states of despair and depression. Seems like everywhere I go I'm getting some kind of message that life has passed me by. I don't know . . . it's just . . . nothing adds up. Here I am, retired, some money—enough to live without too many restrictions—and all I can think of is how I messed everything up. Oh, not really *messed* everything up but unable to build anything permanent. My kids, well—I'm close to one daughter and occasionally I see one of my sons: The other three I haven't the foggiest! And . . . and that isn't right! Been married four times—big deal! What's it all mean now? Adds up to nothin'. I get a little sex every now and then—but even that's a lot of nothin'— no one really cares—no feelin'—just ass, that's all it is. I think life's a dirty deal—all that talk about retirement being the best time of life —let me tell you, it stinks . . . I keep looking back, thinking about Jean—she's the one who got it in that accident. Well, I keep thinking—if only Jean had lived—she and I could have made it together.

Then, the more I think about it, the more sure I am that it wouldn't have mattered if she had lived—it still would have ended in failure. (long pause) . . . I had fun with all of my wives for a while . . . then, well, you know I just couldn't stand them any longer. Honest to God, the other day I saw a man about my age and I envied him—there was his wife and I guess his son and a couple of grandchildren. . . . He seemed contented—you know—maybe not overwhelmingly happy, but contented—like his life had added up to something—like it counted. Then all of a sudden I had this feeling in my stomach—sort of an ache, and then I felt nauseated—like I was vomiting part of myself up."

It is interesting that Howard did not sense unhappiness or self-disgust until later in his life. It would be a fair assumption that there were many good things about each marriage and that each relationship had a lot of intrinsic meaning. The void which has come into Howard's later life is not so much the void due to the loss of a beloved person but rather the void of realizing he has been unable to create or to preserve a configuration of lasting value to him. No meaningful thread tied all the separate relationships together into a meaningful whole. Even Howard's five children lacked a place in the overall picture. While there is no doubt that much of Howard's problem has been in Howard himself for many years, he was able to defend against the emptiness until his later years. No longer being able to do so he views life in a cynical way.

A third alternative has been known traditionally as "group marriage," implying a communal living arrangement. However, not all communal living arrangements imply group marriage. An increasing amount of research is being done on group marriage. The following statements come from Larry and Joan Constantine, who are among those who have contributed to this research:

As researchers studying multilateral marriage (often called group marriage) we find ourselves in contact with developments at the very edge of marriage and family relations. Multilateral marriage is an essentially egalitarian marriage relationship in which three or more individuals (in any distribution by sex) function as a family unit, sharing in a community of sexual and interpersonal intimacy. We feel that the multilateral marriages we have studied over the past year, and related phenomena with which we have had contact, are definite precursors of a significant new social process. [The Constantines conclude] . . . multilateral marriage, though a promising growth-oriented form of marriage, is itself a structure limited to a relative few.[7]

Benefits of group marriage may include greater latitude in individual growth and self-actualization, variety in sexual relationships and patterns, reduced living expenses—and correspondingly less tension and anxiety over financial problems—several parent figures for children, and an in-depth interpersonal sharing. Disadvantages may include jealousy, possessiveness, disagreement about "forced choice" vs. "free choice" in sexual matters, unequal distribution of work and financial responsibility, differing beliefs about socialization and parenting of the children, and the handling of conflict. There are also the ongoing problems of societal pressure, community relations, and economic survival.

Historically, there has been distinction between group marriage and polygamy. *Polygamy* is a general term that takes two forms: either *polyandry,* in which one wife has two or more husbands; or *polygyny,* in which one husband has two or more wives. Group marriage, on the other hand, is usually considered a combination of both forms of polygamy. Polyandrous unions have been more common in hunting and fishing subsistence economies. The several husbands are "home" at different times. Usually, but not always, the polyandrous society desires a low birth rate due to the scarcity of items necessary for survival. Thus, a "wife" has sexual relations with several husbands but the biological facts limit her childbearing to only once every nine months. Polygynous unions have been more frequent in agriculturally based economies in which a higher birth rate is desirable. Polygyny, while often considered the "norm" of the culture, is usually an economic status symbol since few of the males can actually afford more than one wife. Economically successful males are *expected* to take more than one wife.

Thus, a group consisting of three people would formerly have taken one form of polygamy but now would probably be a "multilateral marriage" (current terminology for "group marriage"). That is, because polygamy used to come about out of economic necessity, and because previous economic limitations no longer apply in our culture, it is probably safe to say that people are getting married today for less immediate reasons—to satisfy needs higher in Maslow's hierarchy, psychic needs. Polygamous unions require harmony, not psychic intimacy; today's multilateral marriages seek psychic intimacy in addition to harmony and economic benefits. Research is still necessary in the study of multilateral marriage, especially to discover the minimum, maximum, and ideal sizes of the group. Additionally, very little is known about the longevity and durability of such unions.

Communal families are considered a fourth alternative because they may or may not include group marriage. The historical Oneida Community, under the charismatic influence of John Humprey Noyes, is a prime example of communal living which was also group marriage. The kibbutzim (communal farms) of Israel, however, are not normally thought of as group marriages, but they are communal families. The settlement at New Harmony, Indiana, for both the Rappite and the Owenite periods was communal in its life style, yet it did not include group marriage.

Utopian experiments, including the early Communist familial experiment in the USSR (1918–1936) have not fared well over time. The Oneida Community endured for 34 years (1846–1880). The kibbutzim would appear, from the perspective of history, to be the most successful communal enterprise. "The history of the Kibbutzim dates back to the 1880's when a group of Russian Jews established the first agricultural collectives in what, at that time, was Palestine." [8] Leslie says that by 1936 there were 47 kibbutzim in Palestine, and by 1948 when the state of Israel came into being there were 149. In 1954 the number reached 227.[9] The test of time is one, but only one test. The kibbutzim have been constantly changing and evolving, and it seems, at this writing, that they will endure in one form or another for some time to come.

Communal experiments have been regarded as utopian because they usually seek, in one way or another, to cope with the world by withdrawing from society. Thus, although they may differ in form, they usually have in common a disaffection with the traditional patterns and mores of the society. There is either a feeling of societal disillusionment or rebellion against traditional authority. There is sometimes a religious–theological assumption that becomes the motivating factor in the communal establishment; other communal societies may be based on certain political presuppositions.

Common problems facing communal societies include child care and nurturance, educational provisions, economic subsistence, sexual privileges and mores, internal discipline and government, external relations with the community, and the ordinary problems of day-to-day interpersonal relationships.

In the United States today there has been a notable growth in communal living establishments, many including a variation on the theme of group marriage. The prospects for the successful endurance of these societies appear to be slim. What is probably happening, and will continue to happen, is that people who are dissatisfied or disillusioned, in one way or another, with traditional marital patterns or with the American society as such, will continue to form new unions and living patterns. Some of these will endure. Those that do, in all probability, will reflect a fairly strong organizational structure and procedure. The less attention to structure, discipline, procedure, and continuing governing patterns, the greater the stress placed on the individuals. Nonselective membership and the lack of internal control will likely combine to spell the death knell for many such experimental arrangements.

The backward glance to historical precedents leads one to be extremely cautious about high-sounding predictions. Small group marriages of the multilateral type will probably become the favored organizational pattern for those whose motivation is to seek more satisfying sexual expression. In these smaller multilateral marriages, constant turn-over and adaptation will probably be necessary if they are to survive. If problems relating to child care, sexual expression, jealousy, interpersonal rivalry and competition, and group discipline can be handled in imaginative and creative ways, the possibility for success in particular instances is greatly enhanced.

Nevertheless, it appears to me that a historical perspective combined with a consideration of the dynamics which motivate people to consider such living arrangements indicate that caution is necessary as one contemplates the rather overidealistic, utopian picture of the future possibilities of such patterns. I would hazard the guess that at most 2 or 3 percent of the population may eventually be attracted to such marital and familial structures and that group and communal arrangements are not a viable option for the overwhelming majority of the population. The people who have the highest degree of personal maturity and the highest degree of self-actualizing ability seem to be the ones who, if they were ideologically committed to the concepts of group marriage or communal living, could contribute significantly to their success. Paradoxically, however, these people appear to be the least interested.

A fifth variation in the patterning of familial structure is known as "cluster marriage." Margaret Mead has described this pattern as a cluster of families who retain their identity within the cluster; there is no common occupational or economic base. According to Mead,

> There would be in each cluster some families, some childless married couples, older and younger, some individuals not yet married, some working or studying and some retired, some with strength for energetic play and talk with children and some very fragile persons whom even children could help care for. . . . Some things would be owned personally; other necessary resources would be owned and used within the larger group . . . Nor should families and individuals make long term commitments to membership. It is necessary, I think, for people to keep the sense that they are free to change and move.[10]

The cluster family pattern is designed to help overcome the sense of isolation and alienation experienced by many nuclear families since the "extended" family of prior generations no longer is typical or normative, if indeed it ever was. There are currents of feelings about "aloneness" and "isolation" and "alienation" which tend to motivate people toward structural changes which may help to overcome these barriers and to provide a more enriched style of daily family living. Frederick Stoller outlines some of the specifications of such a cluster group, including a circle of families, regular and frequent meetings, reciprocal sharing, exchange of services, and extension of values.[11] Such a cluster group would necessitate physical proximity, most likely a neighborhood. Families could buy homes in a given block, or subdivision; they could build, buy, or rent an apartment house. Each family would live alone, yet physically adjacent or otherwise close to other families in the cluster.

> Under discussion here . . . is a different arrangement in which families have consistent alternatives before them: to share or to hold to themselves. To have never known privacy is, of course, to be robbed of the experience of separateness. However, to have never known the experience of openness and sharing is to be denied the possibilities of interchange with others. Exclusive adherence to either one of these polarities can only be impoverishing; the individual is faced not with a choice but with a limitation. The intimate family network, therefore, stands for a diversity of experience, a moving between privacy and sharing rather than the exclusive reliance upon one or the other.[12]

Again, as with other structural changes, a fair guess would be that a relatively small percentage of the population will be able to create, organize, and sustain such an arrangement. As a deliberately chosen mode or life style, the cluster depends on too many contingencies. Such clusters do exist, but they have usually evolved *spontaneously* in subdivisions and housing complexes as intimate friendships have developed and the style of interfamilial interaction became a value for the "cluster" of families involved.

A final type of nontraditional pattern to be considered in this section is the phenomenon known as mate swapping, or "swinging." In this arrangement, people exchange partners for sexual purposes only. There may or may not be other commitment or sharing. Mate swapping is not usually considered to imply any communal or group marital arrangement; its structure ranges from complete spontaneity to well-organized clubs, which are advertised in magazines, tabloids, and newspapers. The larger clubs may have regular meeting times with planned games and agenda leading to "orgies." Rules are quite explicit about total involvement and acceptance of every person as a partner. The number of mate-swapping clubs has increased in recent years, and perhaps significantly, it is confined largely to the middle class.

Two couples with mutual interests may have partner exchanges on a regular basis. Advertisements, again, often serve to bring such couples together. Swinging has advantages which group marriage does not have, and vice versa. While advocates of group marriage point out that there is a total commitment by members of the group to each other and to the marriage and that there are rewards to be found in interpersonal sharing, communication, and a life style devoid of routine, boredom, and loneliness, one may wonder to what extent group marriage is a gigantic rationalization for sexual variety. If this is so, then mate swapping would appear to be a more honest endeavor than multilateral marriage. The advantage of mate swapping is that the nuclear family remains intact, and the husband and wife are mutually involved, preventing the placing of a stigma on either partner. Further, advocates of mate swapping claim that feelings of jealousy may be nonexistent or minimal and that if any incompatibility or dissatisfaction exists, the relationship one couple has with another can be easily terminated.

Trial Marriage

The structures described above all have at least one thing in common: they involve unique sexual and marital relationships with other adults who were not part of the original conjugal dyad. Trial marriage deserves to be considered apart from the above patterns because it implies a change in marital status and definition rather than a change in marital structure or any relationship beyond the dyad. Trial marriage is a way of deciding whether or not two people should enter the state of marriage. Whereas the previous section dealt with possible structural changes that have slim chance of ever involving more than a tiny percentage of the total population (despite rampant publicity), trial marriage is increasingly widespread, especially within the campus community. Indeed, it is evolving as a viable alternative to the traditional "engagement."

The following statement is written by a college senior who had kept a journal during the period of her trial marriage. At the time of the trial relationship she was 20 years old and her partner was 22. Her statement is included here in order to give the reader a glimpse into a real "trial" relationship before we consider its various underlying concepts.

Case Study 11

We were to have been married in August, but the date was postponed indefinitely. I wasn't as sure as he of marriage, so since we both were to attend summer school, we rented a house together for two and a half months. Now, eight months later, I can look back through the journal I kept of those days and congratulate myself for having the courage to enter that trial marriage. Quickly, all the disillusionments of the early months of marriage set in—loss of romantic feelings, squabbling over everything, mutual feelings of being taken for granted, and sex becoming part of a daily routine. It was a highly emotional time for me, as I swung from great joy and tenderness to awful depression over what seemed such a failure—us. My predominating emotion was the sense of being "trapped," of "finality." One day in my journal I complained that I felt possessed, and longed for an "open-ended relationship. What I've got instead seems closed, and is pushing me down a narrowing funnel toward a wedding ring." Even on the "good" days when I thought maybe we could make it work, I called my feeling "resignation." I was trapped by love and a "duty" to return that love. Now I can see that my "trap" was partially self-made by my own emotional needs and insecurities.

Our house shook with conflict—over how to fry bologna, when to feed the dog, the dishes, sex—anything! Much of the conflict stemmed from the final uncovering of our *true* attitudes toward ourselves, each other, and life in general—but the fights were usually about the little surface annoyances. Communicating the real gripes was very difficult. Did I love him intellectually as well as emotionally? Why did I resent him so much—was he too dependent on me? At the time, I was too involved to sort out all the problems; I only felt the disappointments. We had friends, a newlywed couple, who were experiencing the same things. I'm so glad that mine was only a trial "marriage" because if I had been chained by a ring and a license, I don't know how I could have handled the intense disillusionment, the unavoidable conviction that we had made a mistake.

At the end, he left town as planned, and two months later I found strength to break our engagement. Now I see that not only were we not "right" for each other, but also that it was not the right season of my life for the responsibility of marriage—I still have much growing to do before I will be ready. As far as the ethical question of what we did, I do not see how we could have chosen a more "moral" action. We accepted our responsibility to ourselves, our possible children, and to society by trying to ascertain whether we could build a fruitful marriage *before* we made a final commitment. *If* we had married instead, and *if* it had lasted, I think we would both be very unhappy right now. Even my parents, who were understandably upset at first, now agree with me and share my happiness at having avoided a costly mistake.

My trial marriage was a time of dreaming, planning, fighting, and crying—a very painful time; but I know that I will never marry anyone until we have seriously tried our marriage on for size *first*.

We shall outline one concept of trial marriage as advocated by anthropologist Margaret Mead, and then proceed to discuss changes, alternatives, and deviations from her prototype.[13] Mead envisions two kinds of marriage: individual marriage and parental marriage. Individual marriage would "be a licensed union in which two individuals would be committed to each other as individuals for as long as they wished to remain together, but not as future parents. As the first step in marriage, it would not include having children."[14] Mead says that the obligation would be an ethical one, not an economic one. That is, if the relationship broke up neither spouse would be able or expected to claim support from the other. The legality of the relationship would consist in a "registration" of the union with the civil authorities. "Individual marriage . . . would be a serious commitment, entered into in public, validated and protected by law and, for some, by religion, in which each partner would have a deep and continuing concern for the happiness and well-being of the other." [15] If the individual marriage proved to be untenable and unfulfilling, the nature of the original contract allows either of the couple to terminate the relationship without the stigma of society. In other words, divorce in the first step of marriage would be very easy and totally nonjudgmental.

The second step of marriage, termed "parental marriage" by Mead, must be preceded by individual marriage: "Every parental marriage, whether children were born into it or adopted, would necessarily have as background a good individual marriage. The fact of a previous marriage, individual or parental, would not alter this. Every parental marriage, at no matter what stage in life, would have to be preceded by an individual marriage." [16] Parental marriage would anticipate a lifelong relationship, and failing that, would be terminated via divorce, but a divorce more akin to a court decree than by individual choice as in the case of individual marriage. (In other words, divorce in parental marriage would be a serious matter and would be subject to legal codes and procedures: This is not to say, however, that today's divorce procedures would dominate, for there is much in current divorce practice that is cruel, hypocritical, unjust, and punitive.)

When a couple decided to move out of an individual marriage into a parental marriage they would obtain a license and, with or without formal ceremony, define the nature of their mutual commitment to each other. Since parental marriage involves a broader scope of responsibilities, commitments, and obligations, the decision for transition from individual marriage to parental marriage should be a deliberately thought through process, made without haste or pressure, and unaffected by romantic overtones or unrealistic expectations. Herein lies the chief justification for marriage in two steps: The "individual" marriage provides a significantly lengthy period of time for the couple to learn new roles, gain marital identity and experience, and shed unrealistic expectations and idealizations.

According to Mead, everyone would benefit from such an arrangement: the couple themselves, the children *not* born to the individual marriage, the children who are born to the parental marriage, the society, and the members of the society who support via taxation the welfare programs, mental health programs, correctional programs, and so on. Marriage in two steps also strikes at the heart of the abortion issue by answering "yes" to the question "Does not every child have the right to be wanted, loved, hence, invited into the life process?" The "yes" answer is found in the fact that a child is born only when its parents have already entered the second stage of marriage, thus indicating a reasonable basis for predicting a mature relationship with favorable prospects for happiness and stability.

In our society it is considered blasphemous or treasonous to discuss the coming of new life focusing on what is best for the parents! Society seems to say that the unborn child should be considered above all else. I have no quarrel with those who say that the child should be considered above all else. I just point out that in considering the child above all else it may be that the greatest mercy we can show the so-called "child" (a zygote—containing only the potential for human life and personality) is to allow it not to be born. The entire issue of when does life begin has never been settled and it is likely to remain forever unsettled. Perhaps the most we can say is that there is a cellular birth, a physiological birth, a psychological birth, and a sociological birth. An academic or philosophical discussion of these approaches to birth will be of little help in dealing with the emotional issues. The vitally important point to be made is that when a child is born to parents who want the child, who have persevered through the adjustment process of individual marriage, and who have established a marital relationship based on mutuality of affection, concern, respect, and meeting of needs, the promise for the child's future is infinitely brighter. The *greatest gift* that can be given to a newborn is a *father and mother who are reasonably secure and happy in their relationship with each other.*

Looking more critically at Mead's proposal, let us confess that the legal-ecclesiastical establishment may reject it totally. However, such rejection would only serve to reflect their state of *rigor morphis* for trial marriage is not really a debatable future option; it is a present reality, *except* for legal and ecclesiastical endorsement.

While I do not see two-step marriage as becoming the normative practice in the near future, it is entirely probable that within several decades 10 to 30 percent of the population will have practiced it. It should be pointed out, however, that trial marriage is not to be confused with cohabitation or casual living together arrangements. Trial marriage is not a short cut to sexual access nor need it be an indiscriminate method for avoidance of personal responsibility. On the contrary, in terms of responsibility to oneself, to one's mate, to one's unborn and born offspring, and to one's society, it would appear to be a far more responsible process for establishing permanent marriages and families than now exists. Trial marriage need not be rationalized on any theological presuppositions, and for this reason stands a better chance of widespread acceptance.

Trial marriage will probably gain definition and structural form through an evolving process, with innovations along the way, until a cultural pattern is established, much as in earlier eras the betrothal became the accepted pattern, and in more recent times the engagement. What seems to be evolving is an alternative to traditional marriage based on a two-step marital commitment, the first step being a trial relationship unburdened with legal, financial, or child-related matters, and the second step being akin to traditional marital definitions, responsibilities, and patterns. If the legal-ecclesiastical establishments do not endorse this change in marital patterns, or at least seek to deal with it in an honest, forthright manner, the trend will undoubtedly continue without them. Marriage in two steps will become a viable alternative to marriage in one step despite the societal-cultural traditions. Again, this is not to say that a majority will be following this pattern within two or three generations. The movement is a college-population phenomenon and it may be that even within five or six generations only 10 to 30 percent of the population will have participated in a two-step marriage.

If, as I assume, we are continually faced with trends which lead to utopian answers as well as trends which continue to cling to age-old traditions long after the symbolic meaning of the traditions has been lost, then is it not logical and reasonable to seek to deal with changing times and traditions in the most responsible way possible? In a bygone day people were taught that marriage legitimatized sex: many people (far too many, one suspects) married so that they could have sexual relations. To marry in order to have sex is a questionable motivation; we can only hope that young people have quite a few better reasons for getting married. This writer is not advocating a permissive and irresponsible sexual expression. Rather I would suggest that the most beneficial trial marriage would be based on this rationale: "We love each other, we have serious intentions and wonderful dreams; we have a bond of affection and a commitment of ourselves. We will live together, faithful to each other's humanness, sharing ourselves—our resources, our minds, our bodies, our being. We will face conflict and differences, and we will use these as instruments for growth and fulfillment. If, after we have lived this way for a while, we no longer feel we can make it together, we shall part. Hopefully, we will know when to seek the help of a friend or counselor as we evaluate our feelings about our relationship. We may not part—we may simply remain this way for a longer duration. We may, however, conclude that we wish to share our lives in a growth-producing commitment and provide children with the love we experience in our own relationship. Whatever our decision, we will be authentic and responsible to ourselves, to each other, and to the offspring we choose to have or not to have."

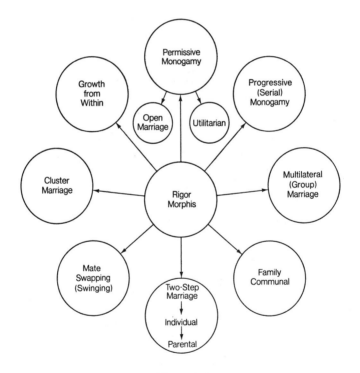

Figure 6–1
Alternatives to Marital "Rigor Morphis"

A Footnote on Trial Marriage

There are those who, because of their own beliefs and upbringing, will condemn trial marriage in any form. These same people will be equally adamant against premarital sexual relationships in any form.

I believe that sexual relationships prior to marriage can be extremely harmful or beneficial. In an age and in a society that has made sex into the greatest idol of all time, it seems to me that the sooner sex is demythologized the better. If, therefore, sex is taken out of the back seat of the car or out of the dorm room and is placed in the context of two people living together and sharing the common facilities of a 24-hour, day-in, day-out living arrangement, then sex is permitted to take its rightful place in the totality of the interpersonal relationship.

The worn-out rationalism "But you wouldn't buy a pair of shoes without trying them on!" is as inept and misleading as the moralistic "sex is dirty" attitude, for when the shoe is tried on it is often done so in a context of romantic unreality, thus leading the couple into a situation where post-wedding disillusionment is far more likely.

Case Study 12

Bill is 23 years old. He has never been married but has been involved in a trial marriage which ended after four months.

"I don't understand it," Bill said to the therapist. "I thought everything would be great. Jean and I went together for about a year and we really hit it off. We did all kinds of things together. I could hardly stand to be away from her and I looked forward to every time we could see each other. Of course, we got close and we had a great time sexually. At first she was reserved but slowly she began to open up and relax. I swear, everything was wonderful. I didn't even think about anyone else—she was it. Even when I was away from her I couldn't imagine myself wanting sex with anyone else. I wanted to get married but . . . well, she wanted to try living together for a while. I kept fighting it by saying I didn't see what there was to gain —that we were like old married people anyway. She really surprised me—wanting a trial marriage kind of thing. Well, anyhow, I agreed and we got an apartment. For several weeks things were fine—but not for long. I don't get it yet—all I know is when we started living together everything was spoiled. Boy, next time I won't try any of that trial stuff—it doomed us. We started fighting—really sort of picking at each other, blaming each other for little things, getting on each other's nerves. She claimed I was closed minded—that I was old-fashioned in the way I wanted to be the protector and the head of the house—you know, like I should let her make the decisions. I suppose I could have taken some of the changes but not the sex one. Boy—how could such a wonderful thing become so dull so fast? All of a sudden it was—like—well, like warmed-over coffee. Before it was exciting and full of challenge—and I really could hardly wait to give myself to her—and man, I mean "give" because it never was just a physical thing with us . . . But, it all went! Here we were living together and what should be the greatest thing became the worst."

Bill, hopefully, will one day welcome another trial but right now he's doing the best thing possible—starting to take a long look at the relationship with Jean. Unbeknownst to him at this point is the fact that the trial marriage saved both of them from the worse fate of entering marriage thinking everything would be just like it was prior to the marriage. In the trial, many things presented themselves as problems to Bill and Jean. However, nothing seemed to bother Bill quite as much as the sexual comedown. In the next chapter, we will consider ways of bringing back variety and intensity to the sexual relationship of married couples. In this light, there is much that Bill and Jean could have learned. Nevertheless, Bill and Jean, convincing themselves that they couldn't make it together, did themselves, their non-conceived children, and perhaps their future mates and their future children a real favor in entering a trial relationship.

---

7   Making It Together: Growth from Within

Are there some cultural marital traditions that seem designed more to destroy marriage than sustain it? In what sense can being taken for granted be good or bad in a marital relationship? Do change and variation in marital patterns need to upset the marital configuration? What are some signs of marital rigidity? What steps can married couples take if they wish to enliven their relationship? Are we wise to expect perfection and uninterrupted harmony in our marital relationships? Is it dangerous to give up one's defense mechanisms? What is left to build a marriage on? At what price do we exact marital fulfillment?

The difference between a "rut" and a "groove" seems to be the difference between losing variety and making constructive use of routine. A rut is negative in that variety and spontaneity have been choked to death; a groove is positive as long as the routine and the ordinary are continually used as springboards into experiences involving variety and spontaneity. People who wish to deny the need of "routine" and the "ordinary" may find fulfillment in one of the emerging marital patterns, but they probably will not find it within traditional monogamy. Two people cannot live together over a long period of time without coming to terms with the routine and the ordinary. The only option (but a most important one) available to couples who commit themselves to a monogamous, sexually exclusive union is the option between the rut and the groove.

To Kill a Marriage

If someone were to appoint a presidential commission on "how to destroy marriage" we could offer some cogent suggestions on strategy. The first maneuver should be to use the mass media to condition people to believe that change and variety are wrong—and to be resisted at all costs. Such a step would allow cultural traditions and patterns, myths, and taboos to be absorbed into a rigidity of form and function within marriage. Isn't it true that we often oblige the commission by commiting "maricide" and "familicide" the very instant we say "I do"? Oh, not intentionally, but in a rather subtle, sneaky way don't we conclude that since he or she is now mine there is no need to continue to score points—no need to be creative, imaginative, spontaneous, or interesting? Many promising relationships begin to die when the relationship becomes legalized—not because a legal bond works some sort of deadly witchcraft but because legalization becomes an open invitation to take the partner *too much* for granted. Our second suggestion on how to kill a marriage is therefore, Take each other for granted—always!

There is no doubt that marriage should provide a couple with a haven in which they can bask in the luxury of not having to put on facades or false pretenses for anyone. This freedom to be oneself provides the joy of being taken for granted, of being loved (agape) "in spite of" one's faults, idiosyncrasies, and hang-ups. Yet there is something in us that doesn't like to be taken for granted, even though we may persist in defending our right to take the other for granted. To be taken for granted is both a relief and a threat; it is both a security and an insecurity; it is both a joy and a peril. Thus, a delicate balance must be maintained in a marital relationship; agape must never be too much out of balance with philos and eros. (In-spite-of love must be balanced with friendship love and physical, passion-filled love.) Whenever equilibrium is upset, it is probably because one or both partners are demanding the right to take the other for granted while claiming that it is not the other's prerogative to take him for granted.

Case Study 13

Frank and Sarah have been married for two years. They have one child, a daughter, age 8 months. Sarah and Frank have come to a marriage counselor because they feel they are at an impasse in their relationship.

Sarah: He just doesn't pay any attention to me. No matter what I do or how hard I try to carry on a conversation he ignores me. He comes home from work and hardly even says "hello." I tried getting dressed up in the late afternoon but he never noticed. When we eat he is silent. When we go out in the car he's silent. Even when we are angry about something he remains uninvolved and unemotional. It's like I'm married to a machine. If only he would acknowledge that I'm alive!

Frank: Sarah makes it sound as though I'm a criminal. Look, I need peace and quiet when I get home from work. All day long I've been selling—sell, sell, sell—and it feels damn good to just turn it off. If I can't relax in my own home where am I ever going to be able to be me? I never did talk much—socially I mean—and if you ask me, Sarah is just making a lot of fuss about nothing. I love her, but that doesn't mean I have to keep on courting her—like I was still trying to impress her.

Sarah: If you love me why don't you ever show me?

Frank: Show you! I work hard for us. What do you call working five days a week going from customer to customer? Of course I love you, but that doesn't mean I have to go around proving it by saying nice things all the time. If you only knew how much I have to sell myself in order to get an order you wouldn't be talking that way.

Sarah: Well it's no joyride taking care of Judy all day long either. All day I care for her, do laundry, cook meals, clean house; and you act like it's too much work to talk to me.

This is a classic situation, portrayed in women's magazines, cartoons, and TV shows. The situation will be accentuated if either partner is especially dependent, because the dependent personality relies on affirmation from others, especially the spouse, for his self-esteem. Even without personality problems, this situation can be destructive if either partner has special legitimate ego needs which only the spouse can fill. For example, Frank's job requires him to be outgoing, aggressive, alert, and "a nice guy." Frank may normally be some of these things some of the time, but he finds it fatiguing to be all of these things all of the time. Consequently, it is natural that he would relish the idea of coming home to peace and solitude. However, Sarah's situation is the reverse, and it is one shared with unknown thousands of young mothers. Sarah has been living in a child's world all day, and she anticipates an exchange of conversation with her husband—even if the exchange is small talk or an abbreviated account of the day's events. Sarah yearns for this verbal sharing; Frank can't abide it.

Thus, we have two normal people who both need to be taken for granted in some ways; but Frank is taking Sarah for granted in a way that fails to take into account her basic need for human warmth and adult companionship. Sarah, on the other hand, has failed to understand Frank's needs after a long day at work. Experiences in role reversal, or in a modified role reversal, could probably help Frank and Sarah develop increased empathy into the situation of the other. Role taking, in which husband and wife practice adopting the other's point of view, can often serve to temper the excessive or unrealistic expectations a couple has of each other. A child can often upset the balance of a relationship also, and Frank's and Sarah's daughter may have made them more sensitive to being taken for granted. They are probably going through a reorientation stage since their child has necessitated a new daily life style for Sarah and perhaps an ego threat to Frank. We have all heard that new fathers are threatened by their children because father is no longer number one. While most men negotiate this adjustment quite well, it is unusual for new fathers to admit that they feel displaced and taken for granted when a child appears.

The rut that Frank and Sarah find themselves in brings us to the third suggestion we will make to the presidential commission: create a cultural milieu in which no one is rewarded for creativity and imagination. Once we convince people that deviation from the traditional role assumptions and marital expectations is wrong, risky, and unnecessary, we can then quickly proceed to the marriage funeral. The rut will become unbearable. I suspect that such a commission would suggest that "imagination" be checked permanently at the door of the (church) (courthouse) (J.P.) (Synagogue)—check one!

Answers to the following questions would indicate that the presidential commission had been highly successful. Answers implying "seldom," "a long time ago," or "we never would" indicate a rigidity in marital roles and a successful campaign to destroy marriage.

When was the last time the couple was separated for at least several days? When was the last time the husband stayed home with the children while the wife went away? When was the last time the couple went away together, leaving the children with a sitter, alone if older, or with friends? Where did the couple go? A nearby motel for overnight? Away with another couple?

How often are the traditional roles of male and female reversed? When did "he" last cook dinner? Does he even know how? Or clean house? Or go to his child's teacher's evaluation conference instead of his wife? When was the last time sexual intercourse was engaged in other than in the bed the couple ordinarily sleeps in? Outside? In the living room? On the floor? Indeed, the sexual technologists have a good point when they lash out at our sexual rigidities and suggest positions in intercourse, changes in technique, and exploration of intimacies beyond coitus.[1]

When has the couple varied the time of sexual intimacy? Must it always be evening, or morning, or on certain nights of the week? When has the couple last reversed the so-called traditional sex-role which assumes that the male is always active and the female passive? A passive male and an active female may be a welcome relief and change for both.

How many couples have ever seriously attempted to learn transactional analysis (see Chapter 5)? How many married couples and/or families use transactional analysis as a means of learning to cope with the conflicts, changing moods, and everyday situations that are common fare in family life?

All of the foregoing questions and statements presuppose a motivation to change, to grow, to explore, and to enrich and enliven. Once a couple agrees to give up, however slowly and gradually, the defense mechanisms and safety devices that they have used to avoid intimacy there is no limit to what can change, with or without outside help. People may protest that centers for development of human potential are out of the question for ordinary people with limited means. Perhaps, although even a growth workshop can be given priority over more traditional vacations or a new car.

Church groups have been increasingly concerned about marital and familial interaction and some have become involved in sensitivity training. It is becoming more and more common for clergy in the more liberal religious traditions to receive training in group marital enrichment. Thus, couples who complain of a lack of understanding friends who might share such group training might not need to look further than their own church, or the YMCA, YWCA, or community educational program.

Many larger cities have pastoral counseling centers where clergymen with specialized training are available for individual counseling, for group therapy, and for marital enrichment groups. Many county and city mental health clinics and Community Chest family agencies also have special groups and classes pertaining to marital growth and family interaction.

But a couple can also work together, separate from an organized counseling group, to improve their marriage. Indeed, transactional analysis is emphasized in this book because anybody can learn it, as has been shown with children, older people, and the mentally retarded.[2]

Two married people can also learn role taking in a matter of minutes—that is, he plays the wife and she plays the husband. Using this format, many conflicts can be dealt with and many feelings explored, for when any one person tries to think and feel himself into the role of another he is bound to have an increase in understanding and empathy. Further, when another assumes my role (plays me) I am bound to get insight and find myself reacting in interesting ways. Others who know us deeply and intimately can give us a glimpse of how we come across to others—can give us feedback. Feedback in human relations can be either divergent or convergent. Divergent feedback is a communication (whether verbal, written, or symbolic) we usually don't want to hear; convergent feedback is welcomed because it agrees with or confirms our self-image. Role taking can drastically reduce the divergent feedback and increase the convergent feedback because it can help one "feel into" the other person and learn to change one's attitude and behavior. More positive feelings (positive feedback) are bound to result from such new insight. Role taking can also help us cut through idealized images of the self and the other by forcing us to see ourselves the way we come across to others. Since idealization militates against a realistic acceptance of oneself and of others, role playing may serve as a tremendous aid in learning authentic self-acceptance and acceptance of others.

Role playing can also help a husband and wife uncover some of their traditional expectations. Thus, a fourth suggestion that the presidential commission should implement is to mount an attack on those who would test traditional male-female and husband-wife roles. The commission should demand role rigidity and a strict sex division of labor, duty, and responsibility to guard against honest self-examination of role expectation, which can often change a conflict-ridden, rut-oriented marriage into a growth relationship. A husband may relate to his wife for ten years on the mistaken assumption that because his mother starched his shirts and cheerfully made a career of housekeeping and mothering, his wife should also be contented to stay at home as sole housekeeper. Similarly, a wife may expect her husband to be domineering and sole breadwinner like her father was, even though she may consciously dislike her father or bear animosity or resentment toward him. Such role expectations, which are deeply embedded in cultural and religious traditions, often provide fertile ground for manipulation of the mate.

A government thrust to "freeze" traditional husband-wife, male-female, father-mother, and parent-offspring roles would go a long way toward killing the potential of monogamous unions. Whenever either partner fails to measure up to the sacred institutionalized expectations of the other, feelings of hurt, anger, resentment, and hostility are likely to run rampant. Thus, a fifth suggestion might be, "Create a national climate that encourages perfection and harmony." A careful manipulation of the mass media could be used to create the illusion that happy successful marriages are those in which there is no conflict, and everybody is improving day by day in their quest for perfect relationships.

Analysis of so-called happy, vital marriages often reveals a total absence of perfectionism and a total acceptance of each other despite character defects, personality flaws, and hang-ups. *Perfection* and *lack of conflict* may yet prove to be the most reliable predictors of *unsatisfactory* marriage—perfection because it is blatantly nonhuman and stupid; lack of conflict because it signals a fundamental dishonesty through denial of feelings.

A final suggestion for our commission (the reader can carry on from here) is to create a marriage ritual law which prescribes phrases of the wedding ceremony that define the marriage contract once and forever as nonnegotiable and nonamendable. Such a nuptial requirement would prevent the constructive orientation that Sidney Jourard describes as "serial polygamy with the same spouse." By serial polygamy Jourard means the reinvention of marriage by the same husband and the same wife. Impasse is struggled with; the old union dies, and a new union is born—between the same two people.[3] The fallacy in traditional marital relationships has been the assumption that people do not really change. While a case may be made for a person's "core" personality as relatively consistent over time, it is also true that we are always changing, growing, reverting, regressing, progressing, or discovering. Hence, it is totally unrealistic to think that two adults should be confined to the (implicit) contract they both agreed upon at the time of marriage. What Jourard calls reinventing marriage is perhaps better described as "redefining," "recreating," or "revitalizing" the present relationship. Redefinition (by that name or by any other name) needs to take place if the marriage is to be a self-actualizing contract for both spouses. Redefinition is an ongoing occurence; the two partners are committed to the fulfillment of each other and to the fulfillment of their relationship.

Perhaps redefinition springs from a certain set of values. If the highest values held by a couple are aliveness, creativity, authenticity, vitality, health, lovingness, intimacy (sexual and spiritual), and productivity, then redefinition will come as naturally as day and night. On the other hand, if the most basic values are loyalty to past tradition, conformity to societal expectation, ancestral beliefs and mores, and the authoritarian triad of obedience, respect, and duty to one's parents, then redefinition will be difficult at best.

The Residual

What remains after we have torn down our defenses in a marital relationship? What is left upon which to build? The residual remains after the tearing-down process has taken from us our defense mechanisms and our safety devices. The residual is the foundation beneath the taboos and myths in which we took refuge; it is the sperm and ovum which united to conceive the marriage in the first place. Many marriages have far more going for them than the partners permit themselves to see. People seem to celebrate failure and divorce by pointing out the things that went wrong—the incompatibilities, the impasses, the drudgery, the disillusionment. Yet at the conception of each union there are legitimate hopes, dreams, and possibilities; there are trust and love, commitment and spontaneity.

What is love's legacy? What is the residual we seek to uncover and recreate? What is it to which we seek to give vitality and fulfillment? The question may be approached in several ways but the underlying assumptions are much the same. Monogamy as it has evolved in our society has tended to work against the development of individual potential; it has tended to create rigidity, joylessness, frustration, monotony, boredom, hostility, anger, and a pleasureless sexuality.

Perhaps the initial step in the direction of change is to opt for a continuing revision and updating of the marital contract. Herbert Otto has spoken of the "New Marriage," which is a framework for developing personal potential.[4] In another article Otto asks, "Has Monogamy Failed?"[5] Both articles are variations on the theme of monogamous marital enrichment:

> Has monogamy failed? My answer is "no." Monogamy is no longer a rigid institution, but instead an evolving one. There is a multiplicity of models and dimensions that we have not even begun to explore. It takes a certain amount of openness to become aware on not only an intellectual level but a feeling level that these possibilities face us with a choice. Then it takes courage to recognize that this choice in a measure represents our faith in monogamy. Finally, there is the fact that every marriage has a potential for greater commitment, enjoyment, and communication, for more love, understanding, and warmth. Actualizing this potential can offer new dimensions in living and new opportunities for personal growth, and can add new strength and affirmation to a marriage.[6]

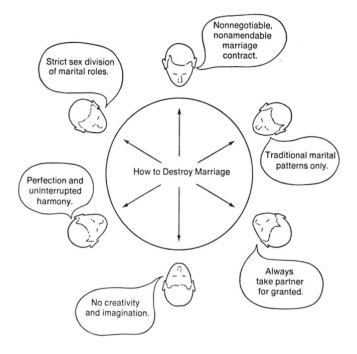

Figure 7–1
The Commission on How to Destroy Marriage

Virginia Satir has also spoken to the issue of "marriage as a Human-Actualizing Contract." [7] Another way of presenting this view would be to advocate the ongoing process of defining the relationship. There are times when marriages peak; there are times when these same marriages are void of vitality and joy. We have noted that the actual wedding ceremony can be an open invitation to decay and stagnation, simply because the two people now legally possess and are possessed by each other. Duty, responsibility, and obligation, however important and necessary, have a repressive intonation and may be cited as the reason for loss of spontaneity in marriage.

Growth centers and organizations for actualizing human potential have sprung up all over the United States.[8] The basic purpose of these centers is to help individuals and couples break out of the binds which constrict the full expression of oneself. In order to do this there must be a willingness to experience some discomfort as one permits the breaking down of barriers and defenses against intimacy. Reawakening of the senses, openness to others, spontaneity in self-expression and honesty in interpersonal relationships are encouraged, usually in a group context.

The history and background of such centers is a story within itself. Our concern here, however, is to suggest that traditional monogamy is still the overwhelming marital pattern within our society and that much can be attempted to revitalize and to actualize the marital relationship.

Yet in defining marriage as a "human actualizing contract" it is all too easy to fall back into the same trap as before—the trap of excessive and unrealistic expectations. Just as romantic and societal expectations often lead one to post-honeymoon disillusionment, so also expectations regarding marriage as the heart-bed of psychic intimacy may lead a couple to discontent and disillusionment. Is it possible for a couple to have peak intimacy experiences day-in/day-out? If the answer to this question is "no," why do we conclude that something is wrong with the marriage? Richard Farson has pointed out that discontent in "good" marriages arises from several sources, including heightened expectations about sexual and psychic intimacy, comparison with other marriages, and comparison of the marriage with itself in its better moments.[9] Farson says: ". . . probably the most important source of discontent is the comparison of the marriage with its own good moments in the present. . . . These peaks, however, are inevitably followed by valleys. Couples lucky enough to have these moments find themselves unable to sustain them, and, at the same time, unable to settle for ordinary moments. They want life to be a constantly satisfying state. But to be a constant state, to avoid the valleys, it is necessary to eliminate the peaks. . . . Good marriages are not like that, but the price they exact in depression and pain is high."[10]

If the residual, the core of the marriage, is to be secured and cultivated it must be tempered with realistic expectations, "realistic" meaning what is considered real in line with what we know about human life through experiences and the testimony of others, including historical and literary confirmation. For example, when Farson speaks of "peaks" and "valleys," he is giving witness to a basic human experience. An idealistic person might say, "Why? Why can't life be filled with peaks?" A pessimistic person may claim in the name of "realism" that Farson is wrong because "life is basically valley after valley with no peaks."

We cannot secure our residual, let alone cultivate it, until we are able to see through the self-destructive tendencies born of unrealistic expectations. As illustration consider the rather common occurrence of a meeting between two strangers on a bus or plane. In a matter of an hour or two, such relationships often yield deep-felt emotions and problems from one or both of the travelers. A common reaction to such an experience is the wish that one could attain and remain in such an intimate level with one's own spouse. But is this a realistic expectation? Can a married couple live day-in and day-out in such an emotionally charged manner? In the majority of bus-airplane instances, the two people involved will never see each other again . . . and they know it! And if, perchance, they do meet again, the odds are that any effort to recreate a semblance of the intimate moment of the past will end in frustration and disappointment.

Thus, the residual has great potential only if it is intellectually and emotionally placed in a context of balance and perspective. If, as we discussed earlier, variety is a desirable quality in human experience, then it follows that we would do well to welcome variety in the range and type of marital relationships as well as in any particular relationship. A couple may achieve a great deal of variety in their sexual relationship, but even this desirable quality will not fill the need for variety in meeting other basic needs.

The residual is, in short, more than enough to sustain the great majority of monogamous and sexually exclusive marriages providing the residual is placed within a congruency of life values and goals which form a configuration. Once the romantic expectations stemming from the media and the conditioning process of socialization are seen through and placed in perspective, there follows the challenge of seeing through the double-bind created by unrealistically expecting our mate to fill all our basic human needs. Let us hope for meaningful peak experiences between husband and wife, yet without either feeling guilty or apologetic about the transitoriness of such experiences. In a very real sense they are meaningful *because* they are transitory.

There are those who will claim that the residual can survive only if the marriage includes the standard of sexual permissiveness. The argument is advanced that if we embrace the value of psychic intimacy with people other than the spouse, we therefore should also embrace sexual intimacy with people other than the spouse. O K for those who so define it. I do not think it is either necessary or logical. What is often desired in sex is an affirmation of the self by the other. It is no more logical to conclude that psychic intimacy must culminate in sexual intimacy than it is to conclude that sexual intimacy must culminate in psychic intimacy. A fair statement about the relationship of psychic and sexual intimacy seems to be this: sometimes and in some situations psychic intimacy progresses into sexual intimacy and in other situations psychic intimacy is destroyed by sexual intimacy. Sexual intimacy often creates only an illusory facsimile of psychic intimacy; that is, when one fails to experience psychic intimacy he deludes himself into believing that sexual intimacy will be an effective substitute. Significantly, a common manner of seduction depends on the manipulation of desires for psychic intimacy as a means of achieving sexual intimacy.

What Price Fulfillment?

The quest for fulfillment comes at a price, both for the individual and the marital relationship. The price is paid in the form of pain and discomfort, the slow process of learning new patterns, the break with security mechanisms, or the parting with games and strategies calculated to manipulate or dominate the other.

The growth toward maturity, toward self-acceptance, toward learning to deal with conflict and unlearning standards of perfection are four specific areas of growth which exact a toll upon those who would build on the residual in their quest for marital fulfillment within a monogamous relationship.

The maturity required to make it together reveals itself most forcefully in the ability to see through the illusions of romantic, societal, and parental expectations of marriage. Further, maturity is manifested in the ability of a person to make viable assessments of the expectations posited for a "human actualizing contract." The more we thirst for the peak experiences the greater will be our discontent with the "down" experiences. This discontent is predictable and inescapable to the extent that we fail to see through the dynamics that we allow to play through us.

Marital fulfillment requires, probably above all other qualities, the grace of self-acceptance. The self-accepting person is the one who is best able to recognize his own foibles and hang-ups without becoming defensive or unnecessarily compulsive in compensating for them. Consequently, he is most free to analyze societal and cultural data and to consciously decide his own level of content and/or discontent. There is little doubt, either experimentally or clinically, that the self-accepting person is best qualified to accept others, most especially his mate.

The myth of conflict-free interpersonal relationships has been treated in an earlier chapter. Suffice it to reiterate that acceptance and confrontation of conflict are essential requirements for human growth and development. Once we accept conflict as an amoral fact of life, we are in a position to be done with old patterns and voices that told us we would not be loved if we expressed our deepest and innermost feelings. In dispelling one myth, we run the risk of falling prey to another myth—the myth that all conflict is resolvable. It is not! To believe otherwise is to add to one's own level of discontent.

Perhaps the greatest price to be paid in building on the residual is the death of perfection. I can hear murmurs and protests to the effect that this villain had been put to death years ago (or at least several pages or chapters back). Maybe so. Likely not! The perfectionist tendency has been reinforced by one's family, competition with siblings, the educational establishment (nursery through postdoctoral), the mass media, and the ecclesiastical establishment. Perfectionism may have been conquered in one or several areas of one's life without having been recognized in one's marital expectations. The purists will maintain that to settle for anything less than perfection is a cop-out or a compromise, yet perfection and the perfectionist fallacy have, in my opinion, been among the greatest curses with which mankind has been historically enslaved. The fallacy of perfectionism is its tacit promise that we will one day be satisfied, when at last we reach the coveted goal. Even if the perfectionist claims he is realistic and that he knows the goal is unattainable but that the meaning is in the striving, he deceives himself precisely because he is unable to live in the present. How can he? He doesn't accept the present without superimposing his own qualifications and improvements. He is then thrust into the future—where all perfectionists dwell—and hence, happiness itself becomes part and parcel of the future illusion.

Perhaps the price of fulfillment can best be described by people who are endeavoring to pay it.

Case Study 14

Gene and Dorothy have been married for five years. They have two daughters, ages 2½ and 4. Gene is self-employed as a proprietor of a sporting goods store. Dorothy is not gainfully employed. Gene and Dorothy record their own story a year after the conclusion of a marital enrichment therapy group in which they participated for twelve weeks.

Gene: I find it hard to think on paper. The past two years have been a whirlwind. First, I was convinced our marriage was a big mistake. I was positive another woman would be much better for me than Dorothy. I have no idea of which "other woman"—I just had the constant thought that there must be a better match available somewhere and somehow. Then I reluctantly joined the enrichment group. I hated it at first. I went more out of appeasement and curiosity than for insight and enrichment. The first couple of meetings left me cold. I know I had a chip on my shoulder. I was critical of everyone in the group, which made me feel quite superior. At the fourth meeting Dorothy put herself in the center ring. I thought, "Oh boy, here she goes in her 'Let's get Gene' game. She didn't. Instead she talked only of her own problems she had been struggling with and how when she was starved for intimacy she would shut people out. I don't recall much else except that whatever she said changed my attitude toward the whole enrichment group. I no longer felt defensive or superior. Slowly I began to participate in the discussions and exchanges. It was very uncomfortable at times, especially when the group members moved in on me and pinned me up against the wall. I guess one thing led to another and I began to get introspective. Then for a while I withdrew into myself. I felt scared and tense. A few more weeks and I began to look forward to the weekly session. My feelings about Dorothy were different now. It wasn't any great turnabout or electrifying romantic episode, just a warm feeling within myself toward both me and her. Somehow I knew that I had been kidding myself about making it with someone else. Sure others might attract me, but now I began to feel that if I couldn't make it with Dot I probably could not make it with anyone. I also began to feel happier within myself, sort of like "a welcome home to me by me."

The year since has not been easy. Many times I have felt despair. It used to be I never felt despair—I guess because I ran away from it. My feelings toward Dorothy have been deeper than ever although, and I can't make much sense of this, we seem to fight a lot more. I express my feelings and so does Dot. This isn't very comfortable.

Sometimes things get worked out. Sometimes they don't. I can only say that even though we fight more there is something better between us than ever before.

Dorothy: It is a strange feeling to put something down on paper that you have carried around within yourself for so long. I don't know where to start. I was becoming more and more dissatisfied with my marriage. Everything seemed to be turning in on me. I felt Gene no longer loved me or even cared. The two girls seemed to occupy most of my time and for a while I guess I escaped unpleasant feelings by concerning myself exclusively with them. The more I allowed the girls to possess me the more I felt resentful toward them. I became depressed and irritable to such an extent that I started to look for help. That's how we eventually ended up in the enrichment group. Gene was against it from the start, but I sensed that unless we did something it would all break up anyway.

The group and I got along fine for a while. I really ate it up. It was obvious that Gene didn't share my enthusiasm. About the fifth or sixth week I started to sour on the group. I felt they were merciless toward me; I felt attacked and I wanted to get out. About the same time Gene started to show signs of interest in the whole thing. So there we were, me against and him for! One night I really opened myself up only to be criticized instead of pitied. It took awhile, about three weeks, for me to look at some of the things people had said to me. More than anything I was wanting group support for my self-pity. They would sooner crucify you than give you pity. My resentment grew worse until one night I told the group how I resented their not giving me pity. Someone in the group looked me straight in the eyes and said: "Pity! Why do you insist that we feel sorry for you?" I started to cry and, of course, I had no answer. When the group ended, I felt about half. It was Gene who benefited most from the group. Since that time things have been better. I seem to be able to live with myself now without being so uptight and depressed. I can't say that the situation has changed any: Gene still works long hours and the girls are still very demanding. Yet there is a difference. I no longer resent the situation, you know what I mean—Gene, his job, the kids, the routine. I don't like lots of things, but I no longer hide my frustration or pretend to myself that some day everything will be different. It's easier for me to express myself to Gene, and when the girls expect too much of me I no longer feel guilty about drawing a line. I have learned to ignore some of the housework that used to bug me, and I've become interested in antiquing furniture of all things. I believe in our marriage more than ever, but it's not a blind belief. I guess what I'm trying to say is that life is better for all of us even though we have the usual stresses and strains. I guess I grew up a little and now I don't need to escape into my "self-pity chamber" as I've come to call it."

This case study illustrates the necessity for the death of perfection. The perfectionist fallacy leads couples to expect the impossible of each other and thus to deny each other's humanity and personhood. As reflected in their forthright honesty with each other in conflictual situations and in their efforts to cut through some of their divisive tactics, Gene and Dorothy are beginning to mature in their relationship. The price of fulfillment does not seem to be cheap; the way is sometimes quite painful and usually uncomfortable. Yet those who travel the road seem to return a unanimous verdict that the price is well worth it.

---

8   A Marriage Wake: Myths that Die Hard

Where do myths about marriage come from? What kinds of expectations have been built up around the marriage myths? In what ways can myths become scapegoats for marriage problems? What alternatives are there to myths about romance, sexuality, freedom, and marital stability?

We have been painting a picture of marriage which may be interpreted by some as less than rosy and by others as a welcome rejection of rose-colored glasses in favor of a clearer view of reality. Indeed, this book is intended to question the value of existing illusions, taboos, and myths about human sexuality and marital relations. This chapter will serve as a summary of those things considered detrimental to marriage and also as a resource for constructive alternatives. Negative criticism is often too easy; positive suggestion is much more difficult, but the results would seem to more than justify the effort. The format of the chapter calls for a division of myths into two categories: *False* and *Half-Truth*. Each myth will be followed by a response intended to shed light on the reasons why the myth is considered fictitious or half-truth.[1]

Fictitious Myths (Totally False)

Myth

A marriage relationship should fulfill all psychological and interpersonal human needs.

Response

False. No single relationship can possibly fulfill the varied and diverse range of human needs. Monogamy makes possible a security-giving dyadic relationship. While the most basic human needs are partially met within the marriage, there need be no limit to "philos" and "agape" relationships beyond the dyad. If the marriage is reasonably stable and secure, both partners may find meaning and fulfillment in many other activities and relationships, both complementing and supplementing the marital relationship.

Myth

Sex is the same as love.

Response

False. Sex is a part of erotic love but not necessarily a part of philos or agape. Sexual love per se is purely physical release. If erotic love (eros) is understood in its noncontaminated, historical sense, it is highly charged with passion, tenderness, the desire to give and to create. In any normative sense sex does not include the totality of the love experience and therefore we are not justified in equating sex with love.

Myth

Love is the same as sex.

Response

False. Except in the case of sexual (libidinous) love. By definition, libidinous love is the physical release of tension created by the libido. For those who accept libidinous love as an end in and of itself, love is the same as sex. However, only this extremely narrow definition of love can qualify to be equated with the experience of sex.

Myth

Sex is always what it appears to be.

Response

False. Sex is not always sexual. Sexual activity is often the most vulnerable carrier for free-floating anxiety. Sometimes it is an expression of anger, resentment, and hostility, or it may be an acting-out behavior through which the individual acts out his deepest feelings and impulses. Thus, sexual desire may be the "cover" for insecurity and a compulsive need for affection.

Myth

Values are a moralistic hangover, repressive and oppressive in nature.

Response

False. A fair and unbiased reading of the histories of Eastern and Western civilization, together with testimony of the existential psychologists, would seem to indicate that when man can define purpose and meaning for himself, with or without reference to duty or supernatural phenomena, he is happier and more self-fulfilled than those who fail to define the meaning and purpose of their existence for themselves. Meaning and purpose presuppose values and a value structure. What needs to be laid bare is the "moralistic" claim based on unquestioning acceptance of custom, tradition, dogma, taboo, and preachments rather than on enlightened reason and learning through human experience. Values which are freely chosen and embraced without coercion are neither repressive nor oppressive.

Myth

Hedonism is always wrong.

Response

False. Pure hedonism is more often disappointing than wrong; it is more often empty than full. Hedonism rarely lives up to its promised fulfillment. The weakness of the hedonistic position is that it fails to integrate the value of pleasure with other values. Pleasure is its own meaning, but it takes on even greater meaning when it is in a congruent position with other values, thus forming a configuration of value and meaning greater than the sum of the individual parts. The value in hedonism is its affirmation that pleasure can be a meaningful expression of purpose when it is not in conflict with other values. Thus, the value of hedonism is limited, but not wrong.

Myth

Romantic love is prosexual.

Response

False. Romantic love is blatantly antisexual, for sex is considered only as an inconsequential by-product of the idealized love relationship rather than as a genuine human experience in its own right. While sexual or libidinous love omits eros, philos, and agape, romantic love emphasizes an idealized form of philos and agape, spiritualizes eros, and denies the libido.

Myth	Conflict is bad; marital conflict is worse.
Response	False. Conflict is a fact of life; it is neither good nor bad in itself. The denial of conflict may take the form of suppression and repression of anger, hostility, and resentment, thus also reducing positive feelings of love. The ability to face conflict creatively and honestly must be learned. The effect of dealing honestly and forthrightly with conflict is an important prerequisite for keeping alive and vital the positive feelings of love, affection, fidelity, and commitment.
Myth	Communication dissolves all conflict.
Response	False. Excellent communication between two people who are not afraid of facing conflict and who are reasonably mature and creative in their ways of resolving conflict may not be sufficient to resolve the conflict. Not all conflicts can be resolved, even by compromise. Yet the conflict need not be dangerous as long as it is not repressed, denied, or avoided. One mark of maturity is learning to accept the things that we cannot change, even after resolute and honest efforts at compromise. Disappointment may be uncomfortable, but it need not be devastating; Aron Krich has commented that "By denying disappointment, all we do is shut out our awareness of the real cause of our pain." [2] The belief that there should never be disappointment in marriage is a corollary of the belief that all conflict should be resolved. These two beliefs are the result of unrealistic expectations.
Myth	Love and hate are opposites.
Response	False. The opposite of love and hate is indifference. A person in a state of indifference (sometimes described as having "fallen out of love" or "love is dead") is unable to experience either positive feelings of love and affection or negative feelings of anger, resentment, hostility, and hatred. This then, is the worst state of all, for it portends the death of mean-

ing in the relationship. The negative feelings can only be understood in the light of the preexisting positive feelings. Love and hate are dynamically related; since love is an emotion that deeply affects the human psyche, it is unrealistic to think that there is no possibility of love in resentment or resentment in love.

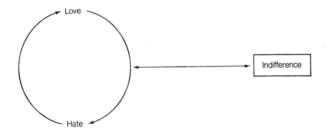

Figure 8–1
The Opposite of Love and Hate Is Indifference

Myth

Response

Man (Homo sapiens) by nature is a monogamous creature. Man by nature is a polygamous creature. Neither belief has ever been established. Early societies were essentially isolated from each other, and their marriage patterns were monogamous and polygamous. In polygamous societies the method of subsistence combined with the desire for a low or high birth rate so that in hunting, fishing, food-gathering, and nomadic societies polyandry was more likely since it kept the birth rate down. In polygynous societies, one may expect to find an agricultural subsistence and a higher birth rate. Whether or not monogamy or polygamy is the "natural" thing cannot be resolved by looking at the animal world, for the wolf and the tiny gerbil are monogamous, while many other species are not. The appeal to morality depends entirely on the mores of the society in which the appeal is made. In some instances, a man would be considered lax in his duty if he had only one wife. The appeal to religious authority depends on the religious tradition to which one appeals. The appeal to libidinous drives and desires for justification for multiple mates may reveal more about man's psyche than about his libido. The traditions, customs, and mores of a given society together with one's own sense of value and meaning would appear to be the more accurate predictors of "man's essential nature."

Myth

Sexual compatibility prior to marriage is a reasonable guarantee of marital success.

Response

False. It is a reasonable guarantee that prior to marriage the couple is sexually compatible—nothing else. Marriage counselors have reported numerous instances in which premarital sexual compatibility did not guarantee marital compatibility. The sexual relationship is affected by many variables, including finances, child discipline, individual autonomy, degree of fulfillment, and general level of marital satisfaction. A few marriages may have an adequate sexual relationship despite the fact that the marital relationship as a whole is poor. The question becomes a chicken and egg proposition: Does a good sexual relationship create a viable marital relationship or does the total marital relationship make possible an enjoyable sexual relationship? Whichever way, one thing is established. The sexual relationship is inseparable from the total marital relationship; each affects and is affected by the other.

Myth

The true sign of sexual compatibility is simultaneous orgasm.

Response

False. The mistaken assumption behind this myth is that sexual performance is the key to sexual pleasure. Of more importance in establishing sexual compatibility than biological acrobatics and goal-oriented sex is the couple's experiencing of each other through giving and receiving pleasure, one form of which may be simultaneous orgasm. However, simultaneous orgasm is more an added pleasure than a standard against which to measure sexual performance or compatibility.

Myth

(a) Painless divorce procedures would be a good thing for the institution of marriage. (b) Strict divorce procedures are necessary if the institution of marriage is to survive.

Response

False on both counts. Strict divorce procedures are unrealistic, punitive, and dehumanizing because they reduce the couple and their children to the state of prisoners of each other and the system. Human growth and self-actualization can hardly be the result of such a state of being. Extremely liberal divorce laws may do the family structure an equal injustice. If divorce is reduced to a mere ritual the couple may never come to terms with the possibility for human growth and actualization implicit in the facing of conflict. Conflict resolution is not an easy thing, as we have seen; conflict resolution requires a looking into oneself which is usually an uncomfortable and threatening experience. Consequently, many people not only unconsciously repress conflict, they also consciously avoid it or run away from it. The option to exit from marriage is important but if the exit is too easy and attractive the marriage will be dissolved without either partner having to face himself, the other, or the dynamics of their interpersonal situation. Perhaps our society will one day evolve into a position in which divorce is serious but not cruel and punitive, not an easy avenue of escape, and neither dehumanizing nor void of commitment and trust over time.

Myth

Marriage is a phenomenon of the past.

Response

False. Variations in marital patterns are on the increase; many more people genuinely choose not to marry at all. Nevertheless, if marriage is a phenomenon of the past, the unmarried segment of the population doesn't seem to realize it, nor do those who have divorced and (while they decried all the ills and injustices of the marital institution) proceeded to remarry. What appears to be a phenomenon of the past is the uniformity of marriage contracts and definitions. The right to renegotiate the contract and the challenge of redefining the relationship are replacing the old stereotypes of rigidity, indissolubility, and unholy deadlock.

Myth

The family is in a state of breakdown and decay.

Response

False. Which family? Whose family? Moralists and politicians seem to relish this theme. The evidence to support it is little different from the evidence used by Socrates and Aristotle circa 400 B.C. A companion myth is "the youth are going to the dogs." In recent years the family in the United States has undergone changes in life style, leisure-time pursuits, mobility, method of communication, and intergenerational relationships. As the function of the rural, economically self-sufficient, three-generation stereotype of the past has changed, so has the structure of the family changed. Is this to be defined as breakdown? Divorce rates are higher than in previous decades. Does this mean that more marriages are failing or that more failing marriages are admitting the failure and doing away with the pretense? The family, in one variation or another, has survived for several thousand years. There is little question that it will continue to survive, perhaps evolving and changing, with variations in function and then structure. Man has a basic need for close, affectionate primary relationships. There are few places in American society where a person may afford the luxury of being totally himself, accepting of and accepted by those he loves and who love him, sharing the joys and sorrows, the accomplishments and the failures of everyday life. No society or group within a society has succeeded over a period of time to effectively replace the family as the primary socialization unit for the young. Even the kibbutzim are variations of family structure. As rigid stereotypes, customs, and traditions break down, the family will be increasingly free to explore new variations and new modes of expression. The family at its best is an emotional base of operations for parents and children, who need the security of being wanted, loved, and needed. From this base, family members can venture forth into the world.

Myth	If women would stay where they belong, there wouldn't be so many family problems.
Response	False. This is scapegoating par excellence! People who are terribly threatened by change would like to endow the past with sanctity and righteousness. The status of the female in any culture is a vital clue to the economic, marital, and familial patterns of that

culture. When women were challenged with maintaining the household and assisting their spouses with management of the farm or other family enterprise there was ample opportunity for her self-fulfillment. Not so today. The female has every right to expect total equality as a human being—equal rights, privileges, responsibilities, and pleasure. There is much to be said for the position that a self-actualizing woman with many diverse interests or employed in some meaningful (to her) capacity can attain and maintain a higher quality of interaction and relationship with her husband and her children. Role reversal may be threatening to the male, but there are absolutely no a priori or preordained role specifications that hold for all societies. Beyond the biological fact that the female carries the fetus for nine months and then gives birth, there is little today which physiologically or biologically limits the sphere of the female.

Myth

The mature person has no hang-ups, problems, or internal conflicts.

Response

False. Maturity is not to be equated with perfection —emotional or otherwise. The mature person can afford the luxury of being himself, free of self-illusions and delusions, aware of his strengths and weaknesses, accepting of his feelings and emotions, and able to identify and label his conflicts and hang-ups. Maturity lies in the refusal to rationalize, play games, or otherwise deny oneself to oneself or to others.

Myth
Response

Self-love is wrong; it is conceited.
False. Self-love or self-esteem is placing a value on oneself as a person of worth. Self-love should not be confused with conceit. Conceit is not loving oneself too much, as many would have it, but not loving oneself enough. A conceited person has never truly loved himself in any meaningful way; genuine self-esteem, on the other hand, precludes any need for conceit. The person with feelings of self-worth, authenticity, self-respect, self-trust, self-acceptance, and self-confidence is under no compulsion to build himself up in the eyes of others.

Half-Truth Myths (Partly True–Partly False)

Myth	Marriage can make unhappy people happy.
Response	To a point—and perhaps for a time. If the degree of depression is medium to severe, it is likely that the depressed (unhappy) partner will drag down the relationship by depending on the spouse to fulfill impossible expectations. Often the experience of "falling out of love" is really an expression of disillusionment and disappointment that the partner no longer cares because he or she "doesn't fulfill my needs" (doesn't love me anymore), even though these ego needs may be illegitimate.
Myth	The trouble with marriage today is the legal-ecclesiastical tradition that undergirds it and defines it.
Response	Partly—but only partly—true. Religious and legal codes are notoriously slow to change, but to ascribe to these codes the root cause of marital disillusionment is to overlook several other key contributing factors, such as the societal expectations, the socialization process, and the personality orientations of the partners.
Myth	The trouble with marriage today is unrealistic societal expectations.
Response	Partly—but only partly—true. Societal expectations arise out of custom and tradition that once had meaning and purpose. When the custom and tradition are no longer representative of reality, the corresponding expectations also become void of authenticity. Thus, it becomes the responsibility of the partners to define the meaning of their own relationship and the nature of their conjugal expectations. Unrealistic societal expectations can then fall by the wayside as more couples begin to define more realistic expectations.
Myth	The trouble with marriage today is the socialization process.
Response	Partly—but only partly—true. Passing blame (and hence responsibility) to one's parents and significant others is an overworked game. While it is true that we deeply internalize our earliest feelings and experiences, it is also true that in maturity we can choose to reevaluate the data we acquired while we were

young. Much of the data may prove to be trustworthy and correct; some may have been ill-conceived and blatantly false.

Myth

The main cause of marriage troubles today is the personality characteristics of the couple.

Response

Partly—but only partly—true. Certainly the two individuals bring to the union a plethora of traits, characteristics, quirks, hang-ups, and idiosyncrasies that will affect their patterns of communication, conflict resolution procedures, discipline of the children, expenditures of money, and sexual patterns. Nevertheless, none of us is exempt from cultural and societal conditioning, tradition, custom, socialization, and the expectations arising therefrom.

Myth

The trouble with marriage today is the widespread lack of sexual savvy and technique, owing to repression and inhibition.

Response

This is only slightly true. Advocates of this myth see the sexual relationship as the cure-all and end-all of marriage. While it is true that a nonrepressed and noninhibited sexual relationship is vitally important, it is also true that when two people are in tune with each other in terms of values, conflict resolution, and communication skills, sexual problems become less crucial. An honest, open, and uninhibited sexual response is more likely the result of a stable marriage than the cause of it.

Myth
Response

Women do not enjoy sex—they endure it.
Since the sixteenth century in Western European societies—partly true. Today—blatantly false as a generalization and physiologically false as demonstrated conclusively by Masters and Johnson.[3] This myth has enough historically patterned conditioning behind it to effectively persuade many people. Not only is it entirely possible for the female to enjoy sexual relations, in many cases the female has been known to be far more sexually responsive than the "average" male. The belief that women—or "nice women"—should not enjoy sexual relations is a corollary of the belief that women are fragile, weak, inferior creatures, whose duty is to submit to the male.

From this belief has arisen the "good girls don't enjoy it, bad girls do" syndrome, which accounts for the fact that some men are impotent with their wives, yet potent with prostitutes or pick-ups.[4]

Myth
Response

Coitus is the only "normal" form of sexual relations. If "normal" means the achievement of union of sperm and ovum, then the myth is correct. If, however, "normal" means the "right" way, or the "moral" way, or the "acceptable" way, then the myth is false.[5] Therapists, marriage counselors, and sexologists are in fairly close agreement that coitus is only one way of having sexual relations; the range of sexual relations includes whatever is mutually acceptable and enjoyable to both participating partners, short of biological perversion.

There are three ways of defining perversion—biologically, societally, and theologically. Since the societal and theological definitions are tied to societal norms, taboos, and religious dogma, there may be great variation in what is considered perversion according to the societal and theological formulas. Therefore, the biological definition of perversion appears to be the most nearly universal in that it considers perversions as those practices injurious to the human body, including such practices as sadism, masochism, rape, pedophilia, necrophilia, and coprophilia.[6] In our society, some sexual practices that were once considered "perverted" and were prohibited by state laws are now starting to be recognized more openly, even if they are not being removed from legal definition and sanction.

Myth
Response

Romance is the highest form of love.
For romanticists, this is true. In reality, however, romance as traditionally defined is an overidealization of both love and the beloved. Whether love be defined as libido, eros, philos, or agape or as a combination thereof, one would be hard pressed to fit the romantic idealization of love into it. The romantic illusion is founded on a self-deluding desire for ecstatic bliss. The idealized lover becomes a mere object, which will enchant the subject—for a time.

Myth

Romantic love should exist in marriage.

Response

If romantic love implies an idealization of the love object and of love itself, the myth is practically impossible to fulfill. Romantic love as a foundation for marriage is ill-equipped to cope with the reality of constant intimacy and interpersonal conflict. A balance between libido, eros, philos, and agape provides a far more secure foundation for feelings of tenderness and enchantment than does the modern day derivative of romantic love. If romantic love is the desired goal, the couple probably should not marry or even cohabit for any lengthy period of time, else the romantic balloon will be punctured.

Myth

Children are good for a marriage.

Response

Sometimes yes, sometimes no. Societal and cultural expectations often prescribe children for their "stabilizing" effect on marriage. The opposite is far more likely, however—only the most secure and stable relationships can stand the pressure and strain of children. A child may appear to cement an unwieldy relationship, but should any child be invited into this world to perform such a mission or to be used in such a way? In bygone days, children may have been considered economic assets. In the United States today they are not. Furthermore, not all couples should have children, especially if they don't really want them or if their preferred life style and career commitments would deprive the child of the security of a stabilized home environment.

Myth

Emotional dependency is good for a marriage.

Response

A play on words here. Emotional *inter*dependency is good—but emotional *dependency* either puts a severe strain on the marital relationship or creates an emotional symbiosis wherein both partners fulfill a high number of illegitimate ego needs for the other and make it difficult for either to survive long without the other. If a person lacks emotional autonomy, he is less likely to work out a fulfilling marital relationship.

Myth

Successful marriage should be a fusion of two identities into one.

Response

A matter of opinion. Psychologically speaking,

whenever an individual fails to attain a secure sense of identity he or she will be more subject to insecurity, anxiety, and depression, with pervading feelings of weakness, helplessness, and emotional dependency. If a person has positive feelings of identity and then "loves" this identity via fusion with another, thus locating the central core of his personality in a relationship outside of himself, he may be endangering that very part of himself which originally made him attractive to the other. Marriage may be a fusion without the loss of individual identity. Therapists and marriage counselors emphasize the importance of individual identity, yet within the context of mutual care, concern, interests, and commitment. Thus, a couple needs to be close but not so close that their identities are blurred. They need to be separate but not so separate that they fail to reap the benefits of true intimacy.

Myth	Legalizing marriage is the first step toward killing a relationship.
Response	This belief is gaining popularity. Every society has a vested interest in the marriage of its young people; and further, this vested interest is primarily with the married couple as the central agents in the socialization process of the offspring. Nevertheless, advocates of "voluntary unions" do not generally accept these reasons as valid. They feel that legalization of marriage implies not just a commitment, but binding commitment, which limits one's freedom. It is likely that persons who feel threatened by legal marital requirements are the very ones who are insecure about their ability to maintain their autonomy and who thus feel vulnerable to manipulation by outside forces. One mark of maturity is to be able to voluntarily choose to delimit one's own freedom in the interests of a relationship. Only a truly autonomous person *feels* free and thus does not need to rely on external indications of whether he is free or not. Such a person will choose to participate in developing a meaningful relationship first and will feel compelled neither to legalize nor to defy legalization.

From another vantage point, we may conclude that the myth is partially true when one considers that the traditional marriage contract suggests a "right to possess" in which case the relationship will begin to erode soon after it is legalized.

Myth   Working mothers create problem children.
Response   Not necessarily. Stanley Coopersmith, who has conducted research into the antecedents of self-esteem in children, says: ". . . we cannot assume that mothers who work and who enjoy working are necessarily rejecting or ruining their children. This study reveals that such mothers are likely to have children who are high rather than low in their self-esteem and who are less likely to manifest anxiety and psychosomatic symptoms." [7] The error which needs to be dispelled is that an employed mother has rejected her children simply because the housekeeping syndrome is not her bag. Many working mothers are able to be far more accepting of their children precisely because their sense of fulfillment has enhanced their own self-acceptance, and they can thus be more accepting of others. A further error in this "dogma" is that the quantity of time spent with children is indicative of the quality of the interaction. This is a manifestly false assumption. Parental exposure time with children is no indication of the quality of the parent-child interaction. Hoffman has pointed out that the most significant variable may be whether or not the mother *enjoys* her work. "The over-all pattern of findings suggests that the working mother who likes working is relatively high on positive affect toward the child, uses mild discipline, and tends to avoid inconveniencing the child with household tasks; the working mother who dislikes working, on the other hand, seems less involved with the child altogether and obtains the child's help with tasks." [8]

There are those who will much prefer the security of holding on to some or all of the above myths—a potent way of defending the ego against change and growth. Others will respond with equal vigor to go beyond illusion and myth in order to proceed to the business of establishing authentic interpersonal relationships. With time and effort the casting aside of marital illusions will free the person to more fully become himself and thus become authentic in relating to others.

9   A Marriage Legacy: Socialization for Tomorrow

Of what importance is the socialization process to marital happiness and fulfillment? What should be the central concern of socialization? What are the components of one's self-concept? Where does the self-concept come from? What part does self-concept play in marital fulfillment? What role has socialization played in forming current sexual attitudes? Does women's liberation pose a threat to marriage? What positive benefits may the women's liberation movement have for love and marriage?

The sex-education controversy has yielded remarks such as: "They're too young to learn about sex and all that sort of thing." "Children have no business knowing the sordid facts of life." "We have no right to put pornographic ideas into the minds of innocent children." "Imagine, teaching about reproduction to second graders!" "Can you believe it, they actually took the little boys to the little girls' room—and the little girls to the little boys' room so that the girls could see what a urinal looks like?"

Such remarks would be hilarious were it not for the tragic state of thinking they represent. Actually, however, sex education is but one aspect of the socialization process, which, to date, has consisted of nonpreparing or negatively preparing children for love, sex, and marriage—indeed, for feeling good about themselves. This negative preparation has been thorough enough to create feelings of shame, self-doubt, guilt, and an overall feeling of worthlessness.

The American society prides itself on its educational system, with its emphasis on achievement, accomplishment, and excellence. The emphasis is on math, English, physics, chemistry, history, social studies, classics, languages, music, athletics, and the arts. Home economics may be stressed for noncollege girls and manual arts for noncollege boys. The missing subject matter, except for some few "health" courses and "family living" courses, includes psychology of personal growth and development, physiology of the human male and female, psychology of human relationships and interaction, sociology of the American family, psychology of family relations, the family in cross-cultural perspective, historical perspective in Eastern and Western marriage patterns, the dynamics of human sexuality, value systems and sexual behavior, implications and means of population control, social issues related to marriage, divorce, unwanted pregnancies, and unwanted children.

I am not necessarily saying that all of this subject matter should be taught formally at all grade levels; perhaps the formal approach should be confined to junior high and senior high. The subject matter is certainly no more sophisticated or difficult for the students to handle than some junior high and senior high school chemistry, physics, and literary textbooks. If the teacher is a good pedagogist and has a firm grasp of the material the student will master the subject matter easily at any level of difficulty. Second and third graders have been treated as "innocents" for so many generations that it is difficult for a large segment of the population to realize that we have succeeded in kidding ourselves about this fact, but not the children. Let the reader who thinks children of second and third grade are "innocent" spend time on the playground or on the school bus, or anywhere at all where children are interacting in play and conversation. Male and female genitalia are subjects of great interest to children. This is not wrong nor is it necessarily right; it's just the way it is. A pontificating censorship will, of course, cause the child to doubt himself, learn a sense of shame, and eventually guilt. An accepting attitude may open the door for communication which will remain open for years to come; the child will also be allowed the freedom to question and learn, rather than repress and hide.

The Self-Concept

The heart of the socialization process is the child's development of a self-concept, or self-image. If a child learns to feel good about being himself he will have made the most significant step toward achieving happiness as an adult (happiness as defined in Chapter 2—a state of being). One's self-concept is a combination of many factors and feelings. Self-acceptance, self-esteem, self-confidence, self-trust, self-possession, self-worth, self-assurance, self-belief, and self-faith are all part of the self-concept. One's successes and failures, social popularity, acceptance by the group, positive and congruent feedback, congruence or lack of congruence between one's idealized ego (ego ideal) and one's actual self also affect one's self-concept.

The self-concept is learned, beginning at an extremely young age. The infant quickly senses that he pleases or displeases others. When he is fed, changed, and clothed he learns about the one who does the feeding, changing, and clothing. He learns that he or she is cold, distant, fearsome, and anxious; or that he or she is warm, close, affectionate, confident, and enjoys being herself. We learn this not by schoolroom methods but through *internalization*—a process by which we internalize what we feel and what we experience, whether it be fear or love, danger or security. If a little child reaches to feel or handle his or her genitals and his or her mother spanks the hand or sounds out the forbidding words, "No! No! No!" has the child learned anything? You bet! The child has learned (if, of course, the parents' behavior is typical and repeated) that there is something terribly bad about the area where his legs come out of his abdomen and, in addition, there is a mystery to the whole thing which he can't fathom. He feels pleasure in touching himself, yet he is told by his six-foot-tall parent that he is doing something unacceptable. Thus, a dilemma is created—the beginning of anxiety and repression and perhaps the cause of later obsession, guilt, and a sense of being worthless.

Many children learn to look unfavorably upon themselves as a result of their parents' signals to them. For example, suppose a five-year-old finds some of his dad's wood and, after finding a hammer and some nails, proceeds to create his masterpiece, a small boat. He pounds nails, but most of them end up being bent over. The finished product looks pretty "OK" in his eyes. He's proud of it. He greets his father at the door; Dad is six feet tall. He displays his masterpiece. Dad says, "What's *that?*" "My boat—I made it myself." "It doesn't look like a boat." Internalized message: "Daddy isn't pleased: he doesn't like it: I can't do anything right!" After dinner father and son go downstairs to "fix the boat up a little." New hull, new mast, new nails! "Now son, how's that—here's a *real* boat!" "Gee Dad, it's neat —but—but—" "But what?" "I didn't make it—you did!" When a child is judged by adult standards the result is bound to be disastrous. The child senses his own failure to measure up. He internalizes, "I'm no good—why else would Dad rebuild my boat?"

This episode can be repeated in the kitchen with little Susan making cupcakes or in any one of a hundred other ways—each repetition being but a variation on one continuous, torture-laden theme: "I'm no good—I can't do anything right—I'm not O.K."

What do children (between 2 and ?) learn about marriage and other sexual subjects? Do they internalize the fact that their father seems to enjoy kissing their mother when he comes home from work (or vice versa)? Do they learn anything when father pats mother's bottom while he is kissing her? Is mother acting as if she is enjoying it or does she seem to be thinking "My, how terrible! What will the child think? Will he now try to do the same thing with Suzy next door?" Let little son model his father. If the parents have genuinely enjoyed expressing affection, little son will have internalized something very wonderful about his father and mother and their relationship. "It's fun! It's good! They kiss—they hug—they pat bottoms—they like each other—they're happy! I feel good about that!"

Children are internalizing every minute of every passing day. They are filing away all kinds of data about marriage, sex, their fathers, their mothers, their teachers. They are also filing away some painful feelings—the hurt of being corrected, put down, turned off, tuned out, rejected, criticized, preached at, scolded, shamed, and forced to say "I'm sorry."

The self-concept is born of our reactions to and relationships with others. The first and most significant others are our parents. We learn to fall into line because it is often painful if we don't. We learn to bury our feelings of anger and resentment because it's too dangerous to go against those powerful persons who feed us and make us feel loved and secure. Sometimes our hostility pops out in a misplaced way upon others; sometimes it's just pushed down further inside. The second way is usually worse. Neither is good.

Others begin to influence us—the nursery school teacher, the kindergarten teacher, grandmother, uncle, big brother, big sister, teacher, and minister (priest, rabbi, guru—check one). The system begins to work. "Excel, achieve, produce, read, play football, play the piano. You've got to get better grades if you're going to go to college." Teachers conference: "Joe isn't achieving up to his maximized potential."

Parents are constantly on stage. Do they laugh together, cry together, get angry at each other, argue, fight, shout, get hurt? Do they smile at each other? Do they enjoy kissing and hugging? Are they always short-tempered? Do they talk *at* each other? Do they fight dirty or in the bedroom where no one can hear them (so they think?). A child who learns how to fight fair is a lucky child. Most parents aren't very good at this kind of modeling because they never learned how from their models, who thought conflict was evil. Many children learn to pout and to sulk by copying one of their parents. Walking out the door when one can no longer carry through is also an easy technique for a child to copy. So is crying: "Look what you did to me." "Look what you made me do!" If you can't get your way, it's always fair game to try to maneuver or manipulate the other. Don't be direct— that's dangerous. Be shy, be tricky. Children will pick up this modus operandi very quickly.

The Antecedents of Self-Esteem

Stanley Coopersmith's research indicates that there are certain identifiable patterns of parenting which contribute to high and low self-esteem. Coopersmith states:

> From the findings obtained in this study it appears that the treatment associated with the formation of high self-esteem is much more vigorous, active, and contentious than is the case in families that produce children with low self-esteem. Rather than being a paradigm of tranquility, harmony and open-mindedness, we find that the high self-esteem family is notable for the high level of activity of its individual members, strong-minded parents dealing with independent, assertive children, stricter enforcement of more stringent demands, and greater possibilities for open dissent and disagreement. This picture brings to mind firm convictions, frequent and possibly strong exchanges, and people who are capable and ready to assume leadership and who will not be treated casually or disrespectfully. . . . From all indications, children who are high in self-esteem are apt to manifest independence, outspokenness, exploratory behaviors, and assertion of their rights; children with low self-esteem are likely to be obedient, conforming, helpful, accommodating, and relatively passive. The child with high self-esteem is likely to be a considerable source of travail and disturbance to his parents, teachers, and other persons in authority, and the child with low self-esteem is more inclined to be overtly submissive and accepting. We should note, however, that persons who are low in self-esteem have higher levels of anxiety, more frequent psychosomatic symptoms, are rated as less effective, and are likely to be more destructive than persons who regard themselves with considerable worth.[1]

The Coopersmith research appears to discredit excessive permissiveness as well as excessive punitiveness and harshness. Further, the foremost parental requirement would seem to be a tolerance for the child's individual expression and behavior. Coopersmith minces no words when speaking of self-esteem and neurotic behavior:

> . . . it seems clear that we are now in a position to provide relatively well-established information of the kind of treatment that is likely to eventuate in high self-esteem. Since low self-esteem has in this report been associated with anxiety and neurotic symptoms, and in other studies with neuroses and psychoses, this is no mean achievement. We should restate in this context of prevention that higher levels of self-esteem are associated with greater demands, firmer regulations, and parental decisiveness rather than a tension-free, permissive, and otherwise idealized environment . . . our study provides clear indications that the individual with high self-esteem feels capable of coping with adversity and competent enough to achieve success, and that the individual with low self-esteem feels helpless, vulnerable, and inadequate. Such convictions of helplessness are learned reactions to self-responses and the responses of others, and preventive measures would therefore seek to reduce such learning situations and replace them with situations that result in feelings of control, adequacy, and competence.[2]

There is little doubt that whether the issue of socialization is approached clinically or through empirical research, the way a child is loved and disciplined, socialized and acculturated is vitally important for his self-concept. The underlying premise is, of course, that positive feelings of self-worth and self-acceptance are the most important prerequisite for happiness and marital success.

Programs of family-life education within the public schools are a step in the right direction, but they are too few and too inadequate to make much of a dent. Arthur T. Jersild has long been an advocate of the idea that *every* teacher should be an agent of facilitation in regard to the child's self-concept.

The approach advocated by Jersild is based on the rather ancient concept that the purpose of education is to "bring out" or "educe" the entire person, not just the cerebral function. While educators would be quick to claim that this is still the ultimate goal of education, the products of the system do not reflect it. A holistic approach to education implies that the human individual in his many facets is the first concern. Not only do elementary and secondary schools lack teachers who are properly prepared for the task of "educing" but, as was pointed out earlier in this chapter, there is a gap in the content area as well. We educate, it would seem, for the chief purpose of gaining knowledge about subjects rather than people, for achieving academic ability rather than emotional stability.

> Much of the information we now have concerning the kinds of problems children face and their capacity for coping with them has come from case work in the branches of psychology and psychiatry which deal with psychotherapy and psychological counseling. But the scope of what would be involved in my proposal goes far beyond the population now reached by these professional groups and involves research that goes beyond the conception of which some mental hygienists have concerning the nature of their work . . . The aim in clinical psychology and psychiatry has largely been to help individuals who have failed to make a comfortable adjustment to the conditions of life. The aim in the program I propose is to help the growing person while he is in the process of adjusting to these conditions, including conditions within himself . . . I agree that the learning of psychology on an academic level alone is not likely to make much difference . . . yet I do believe that a discovery about self that is first perceived on an intellectual level can sometimes initiate a chain of reactions that have profound emotional consequences in a person's life . . . the program would probably make much use of group projects as an aid to self-discovery and self-acceptance. It would mean a greatly enhanced conception of the psychological possibilities inherent in a calculated use of present features of the school's program . . . It would mean that each subject that is retained in the curriculum would be used, as far as feasible, as a vehicle for increased understanding of self and others. There is a rich psychological content, for example, in history and in the study of current events . . . It might also be maintained that it is dangerous for teachers, or parents, to dabble with psychology . . . But let us be realistic. Every hour, every day, millions of parents and thousands of teachers practice psychology and, in effect, teach psychology in their dealings with children whether they know it or not.[3]

Jersild bases his research conclusions largely upon what young people have to say about themselves. His data come from personal essays written by about three thousand pupils, grades four through college, on the topics, "What I like about myself" and "What I dislike about myself." [4] Jersild's basic ideas have great potential if they are implemented through a calculated attempt to face the hard facts of child and adolescent development. An approach which views content as important, but which looks upon the student as even more important could conceivably have a vital impact on the students' emotional development. Teachers already in the field would need concentrated study and practice in their role as facilitators of positive self-concept. Teachers being currently prepared would be required to take many more hours of child development, family development, marriage and family relations, educational psychology, counseling procedures, physiological development, health education, and human sexuality.

Teaching the Self-Concept

This writer advocates that the self-concept be taught in both a formal and informal manner, both in and out of the classroom. As Jersild suggests, the study of history, the social sciences, and social studies may, if done creatively and with teachers who are genuine facilitators of human development, produce side-effect gains in the self-concept. Art work, music, private discovery, athletics, literature, biography, even mathematics can be taught with attention to the affective content as well as the cognitive content. Courses in interpersonal relationships which dwell on the learning of communication techniques and conflict resolution are important if the youngster is to learn from a lab type setting. Role taking, role reversal, and role playing can be taught in groups using games and transactional analysis.

My research in family-life education revealed a significantly positive gain in self-valuation as a result of a one-semester course in personal development, using the family life cycle as the point of departure for the relevant issues of child development, puberty, dating, sexuality, mate selection, marriage, and parenting. When compared to a control group from the same school, the experimental classes showed positive gains in self-concept.[5]

Courses in family-life education or sex education can, however, fall into the same academic mold as the other curriculum offerings. A child can be taught facts about human reproduction and sexual functioning until he is blue in the face. He may master the content, but it is doubtful that he can use this information alone to develop self-esteem. Similarly, a child can be taught theories of personal development but unless the teacher is able to facilitate a personal confrontation between the theory and the student's feelings about himself, the knowledge is of little personal use.

There are many hopeful signs regarding the inclusion of family-life education in curriculum offerings, but such courses are often open only to the "non-college-bound" student. The college-bound student must spend his energy digesting facts and content in order to pass the college entrance exams. Intrapsychic and interpsychic relationships are given no importance in educating the intellectually oriented student! Perhaps the furor over sex education was one of the best things that could have happened. Entire school systems became frightened. Some froze all projected plans. Others withdrew existing programs. But attention was focused on an issue that touched the sensitivities of the public. Probably the real losers of the controversy were those school districts in which the superintendents were breathing a sigh of relief that they had no programs to defend.

Nevertheless, family-life education and sex education is not enough. An interdisciplinary approach is necessary. Such an approach would include the physical sciences, health, home economics, physical education, counseling, and the social sciences, including psychology, sociology, anthropology and history. Specialized "strands" of curriculum and "unit" offerings are necessary, beginning in kindergarten and extending through twelfth grade or the vocational school equivalent. In-service training for teachers is absolutely essential, in addition to formal class work in the dynamics of human behavior.

The goal of teaching the self-concept is always the same—better feelings about oneself, about "being me," "my identity" and "who I am." The doors or entrances into the self are many: personal experiences of disappointment, failure, defeat, success, victory, rejection, acceptance, praise, punishment, crisis, illness, death, divorce, marriage, sexual awareness, mores, traditions, cultural marital patterns, cultural child-rearing patterns, alcohol, drug addiction, smoking, obscene language, pornography, X-rated movies, seductive commercials, family arguments, family dissension, sibling relationships and, of course, parent-offspring relationships. Any content area can bring such feelings out into the open to be talked about. A study of history is rich in societal customs, laws, mores, and taboos. A focus on the lives of famous and infamous people can yield material which is capable of eliciting personal affect. Famous people had feelings, emotions, reactions, not to mention hang-ups of all kinds and descriptions. The study of art and music brings us into affect areas which may serve to elicit deep feelings such as love and hate, affection and hostility.

A study of earth science, biology, and human anatomy and physiology are excellent "entrées" into self-attitudes and self-feelings. A study of historic religions can serve as an entry into philosophical and theological concepts dealing with man's essential nature, his destiny, and the meaning of human existence. An investigation into various forms of civil government may lead one into the philosophy of man's essential nature and into a study of the effects of ecclesiastical tradition upon governmental and legal practices.

Essential to a successful interdisciplinary approach and to an overall "eductive" approach are two factors which only the skillful teacher may keep in proper balance. The first factor is the so called intellectual or academic factor which includes the "content" or the substance of the subject matter. The second factor is the "affect" or "emotional" response to whatever subject matter is being explored. Traditional education concerns itself mainly with the first of these two factors. Traditional therapy concerns itself mainly with the second. The combining of "content" with "feeling" by all teachers, regardless of their area of academic specialty, is the basic challenge of this approach to socialization. A teacher should be proficient in teaching the academic disciplines peculiar to third grade or tenth grade, and in addition, should be able to become a "growth facilitator" in the area of feelings and self-concept.

Parental Resocialization

Parents need a way to maintain perspective in the raising of their families. Informally, there are many ways of doing this—chatting with neighbors, getting away, regularity of "togetherness" and "separateness." However, many parents express the desire for practical training and advice in child rearing—not just child care, but the total process of parenting. Community resources are being used today in far more creative ways than before. Nevertheless, the total number reached is, of course, too few. "Parenting" education may consist of small neighborhood groups or small groups of parents whose children or teenagers are in the same course unit at school. Many such groups have arisen as a result of the family-life course or the sex-education course which the students attend. The parents are invited to a meeting to permit the teacher to share with them his concerns and his viewpoints. Before long, the parents are asking to meet regularly as a group, so that they might have the benefit of the teacher's resources but also the mutual interaction and sharing of the other parents.

Adult-education classes specializing in parental needs and problems are necessary if the socialization of the younger generation is to change in a positive direction. Parents are terribly isolated from other parents; they often feel guilt, shame, doubt, and an all-pervading sense of helplessness and powerlessness in their relationships with their growing children and teen-agers. The effect of such classes, again combining "content" and "feeling" may well be the strengthening of the parents' "self-concept" and overall self-attitudes. One can envision such classes using *I'm OK—You're OK* in combination with Haim G. Ginott's *Between Parent and Teenager* or *Between Parent and Child.*[6]

While it may be protested that this is being done today by YMCA, YWCA, churches, synagogues, and community mental health centers, the fact of the matter is that too few are being reached. The average (if there is such a thing) person may be a church member but an unenthusiastic one; or he may be willing to go to a class for parents offered by the school district but totally rejecting of the same class when offered by the community mental health association or clinic. In any event, parents may be far more willing to discuss and share the questions of parenting than any other single topic.[7] Defenses will go up immediately if such classes are given under the rubric of "marriage enrichment" or "family enrichment." Not only are these titles threatening, they have often proved to be filled with sentimentality and moralistic overtones, calculated to "turn off" those who want to deal with real problems in the context of honest interchange.

The foregoing remarks are intended to be suggestive rather than exhaustive. Let me summarize in five points: (1) The socialization process needs a thorough going over if positive change is to be realized. (2) The self-concept is the key, for when our young feel good about themselves and have positive feelings of self-worth and self-acceptance, not only they, but the entire society benefits greatly. (3) A socialization for tomorrow which concerns itself with positive self-feelings is basic to individual happiness, marital happiness, and familial happiness. (4) The educational establishment is in the best overall position to be the chief instrumental agent of change after age five.

This, however, requires far more effort from the school board, the public, and the teacher than is now put forth. (5) The financial outlay (and hence the tax cost) will be phenomenal in the case of teacher-education and teacher in-service training. The cost, however, could well prove to be a bargain when alternatives are considered, such as private therapy, community mental health agencies, hospitals and other institutions for the mentally ill, reformatories, prisons, and, last but not least, welfare. The proposals contained in this chapter are no panaceas, but are intended to undergird the socialization process. Results would have to be measured in longitudinal studies extending over two, three, and four generations.

An Afterword

In its simplest terms, the marriage legacy is a tradition; as with any tradition or custom, its value and purpose may be lost during the process of transmission. When this happens the recipients of the legacy may find themselves enslaved by the legacy and its failure to convey meaning and purpose. When confronted with a worn-out tradition, there are three options: (1) accept the legacy, lock, stock, and barrel; (2) reject the legacy and rebel against it; (3) rework the legacy —reshape, recreate, and redefine it.

In the foregoing chapters I have attempted to carry out option three. Options one and two appear to me to be nonliberating positions. (The person who feels so constrained about marriage and consequently rejects the entire legacy is certainly not a liberated person; he is rather a prisoner of his own disgust and hostility.) Option three, recreating and redefining the legacy, requires individuals who are first committed to winning their own autonomy. Only then, as I have said in earlier chapters, will the individual be able to know himself or herself well enough to separate legitimate ego needs from illegitimate ego needs and to build a fulfilling marital relationship.

Among the conclusions that have impressed themselves upon me as I have treated the material in the foregoing pages are the following:

1. Prophets of doom and prophets of utopian panaceas are both off base.[8] While both should be given a fair hearing, it is vital to exercise critical judgment as these positions are evaluated. A sense of historical perspective combined with a sober commitment to future generations leads me to conclude that the most fruitful progress in

marriage depends upon our ability to reject panaceas and prognostications of futility in favor of the slower and perhaps more painful way of redefinition and concentration on intrapsychic and interpsychic dynamics.

2. Varieties of marital and familial structures are here to stay. The only critical issue is the establishment of the individual's right to define whether or not any kind of marriage is desirable and, if so, what kind of marriage it should be. As I have indicated, there will always be at least a small percentage who will opt for the group structures and for a total permissiveness within monogamous unions. This is a development that need not be feared; indeed, it should be encouraged and welcomed by those who, in their own lives, do not choose those particular paths.

3. Sexual liberation is not a simple matter of discarding Victorian taboos and inhibitions. The truly liberated are those who, in the exercise of freedom, are not enslaved by their freedom. Sexual liberation implies not only a demythologized sexual stance but also a deidolization of sex. The commanding power of sex has been given equal expression in the repression of the Victorians and in the permissive hedonism of the sixties and early seventies. We can be enslaved not only by what we submit to but equally as much by what we reject. In growing out of Victorian practices and attitudes, we may still be sexually enslaved by the total celebration of the very thing we rejected; hence there is only a shift from a negative enslavement to a positive enslavement. In both cases, sex is enshrined on a pedestal and the individual is in bondage.

4. Similarly, human emancipation from restrictive dogmatic positions of the past is not a simple matter of rejecting authoritarian prescriptions. Here again we run the risk of becoming enslaved by the very thing we reject. The tradition of humanistic ethics has much to recommend itself to today's generation, especially to those who have experienced the uncertainty of developing their personal ethical codes upon discovering that traditional codes no longer work for them. Of course, man's search for meaning and purpose is not a modern phenomenon, nor have dogmatic answers always held sway. Authoritarian and humanistic traditions have existed both within and without Christendom. The specific danger to which I am here referring is the danger of total rejection of both authoritarian and humanistic traditions. Rejection of the authoritarian tradition need not lead to a rejec-

tion of the best humanistic thinking embedded in the history of Western or Eastern civilization.

5. Throughout these pages I have called attention to the inadequacy of the English word "love." As long as we insist on dealing with subjects such as marriage, mate selection, family, sex, sexuality, and romance in terms of this single four-letter word we will be unable to adequately conceptualize the problems of each area of human fulfillment. I have employed the language of the Greeks and, following Rollo May, have attempted to give content to four types of love: libido, eros, philos, and agape. I fail to see any other viable way to get at the dynamics of the interpersonal sexual, marital, and familial relationships. The romantic tradition has militated against such an analysis and synthesis of love. Let it be said that the rejection of *romanticism* need not imply a lack of emotion and tenderness in the relationship between the sexes. The excitement and passion of eros sufficiently captures the root meaning of romance such that the death of *romanticism* need not give cause for grief.

6. The emphasis on conflict facing and conflict resolution seems to me to be a most vital clue to successful marriage. Yet, within our society conflict has been a taboo word carrying a connotation of evil, impropriety, and sin. I have attempted to show the importance of dealing first with intrapsychic conflict in order to learn to face interpsychic conflict. As important as conflict resolution is to personal and marital happiness, we should guard against the tendency to make it a superanswer! The importance of conflict is not in conflict resolution per se, but rather in facing and handling the conflict. There is conflict present in practically every human relationship; it is inevitable. We feed on illusion if we allow ourselves to naively believe that all conflicts can or ought to be resolved. Indeed, to the extent we embrace the concept of the individual's right to self-fulfillment we may continue to live with conflict that, at heart, is not resolvable.

7. The interaction of women's liberation, human sexuality, and interpersonal oneness is far more subtle and dynamically volatile than our society is presently prepared to admit. The heart of women's liberation is the issue of humanity vs. dehumanity. When either sex is "up" or "down," both sexes are dehumanized and alienated from each other. Female dehumanization tends to be disguised by culturally patterned rituals which make the female either into an object of adoration (a sex object or sex symbol) and/or into an object in need of protection "for her own good." In either case, the female is relegated to

an inferior status resembling a "china doll"—beautiful, but brainless and nonhuman. This tends to perpetuate the process of mutual dehumanization, since any unrealistic valuation of a human being will inevitably lead to possessiveness and manipulation by both sexes. Things are possessed; people are loved. Love which attempts to possess is not love but bondage. Love is always the child of freedom. A total union or oneness between a man and a woman includes both psychic and sexual intimacy. This intimacy is simply not possible unless the two people are free to embrace the humanity of each other. Thus, a unisex emphasis is a cop-out. Likewise, any undue emphasis on the part of male or female which tends to make the body into an object is nothing more than a perpetuation of the alienation between the sexes which resulted from the belief that one was superior to the other. I would conclude by saying that in love and in marriage neither man nor woman can be liberated or human alone; either both are enslaved or both are free.

8. The emphasis on self-fulfillment and self-actualization is a welcome part of the quest for meaning in human existence. This beneficial concept can become, however, a panacea capable of creating pain and grief if self-fulfillment becomes a pseudo-god such that any delimitation of my personal freedom implies a frustration of my self-actualization. Suffice it to say that two or more people cannot live together in any definition of the married state without each one voluntarily accepting a partial delimitation of his or her own behavioral freedom (as opposed to psychic "inner freedom" which need not be affected by marriage). This delimitation may mean that self-fulfillment is also partially delimited. Further, one's quest for self-fulfillment may lead to frustration if it is allowed to give rise to a set of expectations that are clearly unrealistic. The expectation of highly charged intimacy as an ongoing, continuous phenomenon is clearly unrealistic. I am concerned here that we do not allow intimacy fulfillment expectations to frustrate us as did the romantic expectations bequeathed to us throughout the socialization process. If the agent of liberation (self-fulfillment and marital fulfillment) becomes, due to excessive and unrealistic expectation, an agent of excessive frustration, then the gain may prove to be merely illusory.

9. The emphasis on the socialization process is, in my opinion, the key to the future of human happiness, including marital and familial happiness. The difficulty implicit in this concept is that it is neither strikingly bold nor brilliantly utopian. This means that those longing

for utopian panaceas are bound to walk away disappointed and perhaps disillusioned. But here I must appeal to history as my witness: Panaceas have never worked! The search for magical, enthralling, spectacular, radical answers to the question of socialization for happiness have usually ended in disillusionment. Social scientists, psychologists, psychiatrists, and educators are presently widely divided in their beliefs, attitudes, and prescriptions for human socialization. Divided as they are amidst conflicting theories and programs, there is simply no other alternative than to keep searching, continue doing research, and remain on the hard narrow path which seeks to humanize every person, every relationship, and every institution.

Notes

Chapter 1   [1] "To Make Divorce Less Painful" (Editorial), *Louisville Courier-Journal* (June 28, 1971), Louisville, Kentucky, p. A–6. Reprinted by permission. [2] From Andreas Capellanus, *The Art of Courtly Love,* Abridged and edited by Frederick W. Locke (New York: Columbia University Press, 1941). Reprinted by permission. [3] From Albert Ellis, *American Sexual Tragedy* (New York: Lyle Stuart, Inc., 1962), pp. 97–121. Reprinted by permission.   [4] See Erik Erikson, *Childhood and Society* (New York: W. W. Norton, 1950).   [5] See Erich Fromm, *Man for Himself* (New York: Holt, Rinehart and Winston, 1947), pp. 75–89.   [6] From Talcott Parsons, "The Superego and the Theory of Social Systems," in Talcott Parsons, Robert F. Bales, and Edward A. Shils, *Working Papers in the Theory of Action* (New York: The Free Press, 1953), pp. 13–28. Reprinted by permission.   [7] See Fromm, *op. cit.,* Chapter 2.   [8] See Karen Horney, *Our Inner Conflicts* (New York: W. W. Norton, 1945), especially Chapter 3, "Moving toward People."   [9] *Ibid.,* Chapter 4.   [10] Fromm, *op. cit.,* p. 73 (paperback edition).   [11] Horney, *op. cit.,* Chapter 5.   [12] Fromm, *op. cit.,* p. 75 (paperback edition).   [13] Rollo May, *Man's Search for Himself* (New York: W. W. Norton, 1953), p. 52 (Signet paperback edition). Reprinted by permission.

Chapter 2   [1] From W. T. Jones, *A History of Western Philosophy* (New York: Harcourt Brace Jovanovich, 1952), pp. 219, 233. Reprinted by permission.   [2] From Abraham Maslow, *Toward a Psychology of Being,* 2nd edition (Princeton, N.J.: Van Nostrand Company, 1962), p. 24, italics mine. Reprinted by permission.   [3] From Aron Krich and Sam Blum, "Marriage and the Mystique of Romance," *Redbook* (November 1970). Reprinted by permission.   [4] From Erich Fromm, *The Art of Loving* (New York: Harper and Row, 1956), pp. 40–41 (Harper Colophon). Reprinted by permission.   [5] Erich Fromm has treated the subject in Chapter 2 of *The Art of Loving* and in Chapter 5 of *Escape from Freedom* (New York: Holt, Rinehart and Winston, 1941).   [6] From Karen Horney, *The Neurotic Personality of Our Time* (New York: W. W. Norton, 1937), Chapter 4. Reprinted by permission.   [7] Karen Horney has amplified her remarks throughout three chapters in *The Neurotic Personality of Our Time.* See Chapter 6, "The Neurotic Need for Affection," Chapter 7, "Further Characteristics of the Neurotic Need for Affection," and Chapter 9, "The Role of Sexuality in the Neurotic Need for Affection."   [8] See Abraham H. Maslow, "A Theory of Human Motivation," *Psychological Review,* 1943, **50,** 370–396. Quotations from this article are reprinted by permission.   [9] *Ibid.*   [10] See William Glasser, *Reality Therapy* (New York: Harper and Row, 1965).   [11] See Eric Berne, *Games People Play* (New York: Grove Press, 1964) and Thomas Harris, *I'm OK—You're OK* (New York: Harper and Row, 1967).   [12] Fromm, *The Art of Loving,* p. 26.   [13] *Ibid.,* p. 28.   [14] See Stanley Coopersmith, *The Antecedents of Self-Esteem* (San Francisco: W. H. Freeman and Company, 1967), especially Chapters 2 and 13.   [15] See Chapter 2 on "Self-Love" in *The Art of Loving.*   [16] The list includes Everett Shostrom, Rollo May, Eric Berne, Thomas Harris, Virginia Satir, Harry Stack Sullivan, Karen Horney, Abraham Maslow, William Glasser, Erik H. Erikson, and Andras Angyal.   [17] From Harry F. Harlow, "The Nature of Love," *American Psychologist,* 1958, **13,** 673–685. Reprinted by permission.   [18] From Abraham Maslow, *Toward a Psychology of Being* (Princeton, N.J.: Van Nostrand Company, 1962), pp. 42–43. Reprinted by permission.   [19] See Fromm, *The Art of Loving,* p. 23. Reprinted by permission. For similar thoughts, see Allan Fromme, *The Ability to Love* (North Hollywood, Ca.: Wilshire Book Co., 1966).

Chapter 3   [1] From Viktor Frankl, *Man's Search for Meaning* (New York: Washington Square Press, 1963), p. 159. Reprinted by permission.   [2] *Ibid.,* pp. 153–154,

164.   ³ See Karen Horney, *The Neurotic Personality of Our Time* (New York: W. W. Norton, 1937), Chapter 9. Reprinted by permission.   ⁴ See Erich Fromm, *Man for Himself* (New York: Holt, Rinehart and Winston, 1947), Chapter 4. Reprinted by permission.   ⁵ *Ibid.*   ⁶ From Rollo May, *Love and Will* (New York: W. W. Norton, 1969), pp. 105–109 (selected). Reprinted by permission.   ⁷ Frankl, *op. cit.*, p. 170.   ⁸ From Paul Tillich, *The Courage to Be* (New Haven, Conn.: Yale University Press, 1952), p. 57. Reprinted by permission.   ⁹ *Ibid.*, p. 62.   ¹⁰ *Ibid.*, p. 50.   ¹¹ *Ibid.*, p. 76.   ¹² *Ibid.*   ¹³ May, *op. cit.*, p. 39.

Chapter 4   ¹ From Hugo Beigel, "Romantic Love," *American Sociological Review*, 1951, XIV, 3, 326–334. Reprinted by permission.   ² *Ibid.*   ³ *Ibid.*   ⁴ *Ibid.*   ⁵ From Albert Ellis, *American Sexual Tragedy* (New York: Lyle Stuart, 1962), pp. 97–121. Reprinted by permission.   ⁶ *Ibid.*   ⁷ *Ibid.*   ⁸ See Donald Horton, "The Dialogue of Courtship in Popular Songs," *American Journal of Sociology*, 1957, 62, 569–578.   ⁹ Rollo May, *Love and Will* (New York: W. W. Norton, 1969), pp. 45–46. Reprinted by permission.   ¹⁰ See Ira L. Reiss, *Premarital Sexual Standards in America* (New York: The Macmillan Company, 1960).   ¹¹ For a theoretical treatment of some of these questions, see William J. Goode, "The Theoretical Importance of Love," *American Sociological Review*, 1959, 24, 38–47.   ¹² Ellis, *op. cit.*   ¹³ May, *op. cit.*, p. 65.   ¹⁴ *Ibid.*, pp. 73–74.   ¹⁵ See Albert Ellis, *Sex without Guilt* (New York: Lyle Stuart, 1958), pp. 51–65.

Chapter 5   ¹ Rollo May, *Love and Will* (New York: W. W. Norton, 1969), p. 148. Reprinted by permission.   ² From George R. Bach and Peter Wyden, *The Intimate Enemy* (New York: William Morrow and Company, 1969), Chapter 1. Reprinted by permission.   ³ From Viktor Frankl, *Man's Search for Meaning* (New York: Washington Square Press, 1959), p. 160 (paperback).   ⁴ Virginia Satir, "Marriage as a Human-Actualizing Contract" and Herbert A. Otto, "The New Marriage: Marriage as a Framework for Developing Personal Potential," in Herbert A. Otto, *The Family in Search of a Future* (New York: Appleton-Century-Crofts, 1970).   ⁵ Eric Berne, *Games People Play* (New York: Grove Press, 1964).   ⁶ From Thomas A. Harris, *I'm OK—You're OK* (New York: Harper and Row, 1967), p. 18. Reprinted by permission.   ⁷ *Ibid.*, pp. 18–19.   ⁸ *Ibid.*, p. 20.   ⁹ *Ibid.*, p. 25.   ¹⁰ *Ibid.*, p. 26.   ¹¹ *Ibid.*, p. 29.   ¹² *Ibid.*, p. 32.   ¹³ *Ibid.*, p. 43.   ¹⁴ *Ibid.*, p. 46.   ¹⁵ *Ibid.*, pp. 48–49.   ¹⁶ *Ibid.*, p. 50.   ¹⁷ *Ibid.*, p. 52.   ¹⁸ See Karen Horney, *Our Inner Conflicts* (New York: W. W. Norton, 1945), Chapters 3, 4, and 5.   ¹⁹ Everett L. Shostrom, *Man the Manipulator* (Nashville, Tenn.: Abingdon Press, 1967), Chapter 3.   ²⁰ Harris, *op. cit.*, pp. 126–127.

Chapter 6   ¹ George P. Murdock, *Social Structure* (New York: The Macmillan Company, 1949), p. 264.   ² II Samuel 11:16; 12:9 (Revised Standard Version).   ³ Genesis 16:1–6; Genesis 30:1–12 (RSV).   ⁴ From Edward C. Hobbs, "An Alternate Model from a Theological Perspective," in Herbert A. Otto (Ed.), *The Family in Search of a Future* (New York: Appleton-Century-Crofts, 1970), p. 37. Reprinted by permission.   ⁵ John F. Cuber and Peggy B. Haroff, *The Significant Americans* (New York: Appleton-Century-Crofts, 1965).   ⁶ For further elaboration on open marriage, see George and Nena O'Neill's book: *Open Marriage: A New Life Style for Couples* (New York: M. Evans and Company, 1972).   ⁷ Larry Constantine and Joan Constantine, "Where Is Marriage Going?" *The Futurist* (April 1970). Reprinted by permission.   ⁸ From Gerald Leslie, *The Family in Social Context* (New York: Oxford University Press, 1968), p. 143. Reprinted by permission.   ⁹ *Ibid.*   ¹⁰ From Margaret Mead, "New Design for Family Living," *Redbook* (October 1970). Reprinted by permission.   ¹¹ From Frederick Stoller, "The Intimate Network of Families as a New Structure," in Otto, *op. cit.*, pp. 145–159.   ¹² *Ibid.*, p. 158.   ¹³ See Margaret Mead, "Marriage in Two Steps," *Redbook* (July 1966). Quotations from this article are reprinted by permission.   ¹⁴ *Ibid.*   ¹⁵ *Ibid.*   ¹⁶ *Ibid.*

Chapter 7   ¹ See Albert Ellis, "The Folklore of Marital Relations—The Great Coital Myth," in *American Sexual Tragedy* (New York: Lyle Stuart,

1962).   [2] Thomas Harris, *I'm OK—You're OK* (New York: Harper and Row, 1967), pp. xvi–xix, 170–177.   [3] See Sidney M. Jourard, "Reinventing Marriage: The Perspective of a Psychologist," in Herbert A. Otto (Ed.), *The Family in Search of a Future* (New York: Appleton-Century-Crofts, 1970).   [4] Otto, *op. cit.,* Chapter 10.   [5] See Herbert A. Otto, "Has Monogamy Failed?" *Saturday Review* (April 25, 1970). The quotation from this article is reprinted by permission.   [6] *Ibid.,* p. 23.   [7] See Virginia Satir, "Marriage as a Human-Actualizing Contract," in Otto, *op. cit.,* pp. 57–66.   [8] See pp. 201–204 in Otto, *op. cit.,* for a list of such centers.   [9] See Richard Farson, "Why Good Marriages Fail," *McCall's* (October 1971), pp. 110ff. The quotation from this article is reprinted by permission.   [10] *Ibid.,* p. 170.

Chapter 8   [1] *Myth:* For the purposes of this discussion, a myth is considered to be "One of the fictions or half-truths forming part of the ideology of a society . . . A notion based more on tradition or convenience than on fact; a received idea." From *The American Heritage Dictionary of the English Language* (New York: Houghton Mifflin Company and American Heritage Publishing Company, 1969), p. 869.   [2] From Aron Krich, "Marriage and the Mystique of Romance," *Redbook* (November 1970).   [3] See William H. Masters and Virginia Johnson, *Human Sexual Response* (Boston: Little, Brown, and Company, 1966), pp. 45–67.   [4] See Martha Wolfenstein and Nathan Leites, "The Good–Bad Girl," in *Movies, a Psychological Study* (New York: The Free Press, 1950).   [5] See the chapter on "The Great Coital Myth" in Albert Ellis, *American Sexual Tragedy* (New York: Lyle Stuart, 1962).   [6] See Lloyd Saxton, *The Individual, Marriage, and the Family* (Belmont, Ca.: Wadsworth Publishing Company, 1968), pp. 140–152.   [7] From Stanley Coopersmith, *The Antecedents of Self-Esteem* (San Francisco: W. H. Freeman and Company, 1967), 252–253. Reprinted by permission.   [8] From Lois Wladis Hoffman, "Effects of Maternal Employment on the Child," *Child Development,* 1961, **32,** 187–197. Reprinted by permission.

Chapter 9   [1] From Stanley Coopersmith, *The Antecedents of Self-Esteem* (San Francisco: W. H. Freeman and Company, 1967), pp. 252–253. Reprinted by permission.   [2] *Ibid.,* p. 261.   [3] From Arthur T. Jersild, "Self-understanding in Childhood and Adolescence," *The American Psychologist,* 1951, **6,** 122–126 (selected). Reprinted by permission.   [4] See Arthur T. Jersild, *In Search of Self* (New York: Teachers College Press, Columbia University, 1952).   [5] See John F. Crosby, "The Effects of Family Life Education on the Values and Attitudes of Adolescents," *The Family Coordinator,* 1971, **20,** 137–140.   [6] Haim G. Ginott, *Between Parent and Teenager* (New York: The Macmillan Company, 1969). See also Ginott's *Between Parent and Child* (New York: The Macmillan Company, 1965).   [7] An important book which may encourage a lessening of irrational guilt feelings peculiar to many parents is *Parents in Modern America,* by E. E. LeMasters (Homewood, Ill.: The Dorsey Press, 1970).   [8] See, for example, David Cooper, *The Death of the Family* (New York: Random House, Vintage Press, 1970) and the utopians who advocate a complete swing to communal experiments and group marriage.

Index

Books of Related Interest

The Individual, Marriage, and the Family, Second Edition

Lloyd Saxton, College of San Mateo

    Lloyd Saxton is an experienced marriage counselor and teacher of marriage and the family courses. His bestselling text on dating, marriage, and familial relations has been updated in this edition to include material on the "Sexual Revolution" and the economics of marriage. (503 pages. 6½ x 9¼. Clothbound. Teacher's Manual available.)

Contents

Also by Lloyd Saxton:

The Individual, Marriage, and the Family: Current Perspectives

This companion work is a collection of recent articles that parallel the subject matter of Saxton's textbook and are designed for use in the functional marriage course. There are annotated bibliographies for each section, and test items are available. (515 pages. 7 x 8. Paperbound.)